Pet Owner's Guide to
THE
POODLE

Barbara Cherry

New York
Maxwell Macmillan Canada
Toronto
Maxwell Macmillan International
New York   Oxford   Singapore   Sydney

Howell Book House
Macmillan Publishing Company
866 Third Avenue
New York, NY 10022

Maxwell Macmillan Canada, Inc.
1200 Eglinton Avenue East
Suite 200
Don Mills, Ontario M3C 3N1

Printed in Hong Kong

Macmillan Publishing Company is part of the Maxwell Communication Group of Companies.

Library of Congress Cataloging-in-Publication Data

Cherry, Barbara.
Pet owner's guide to the poodle / by Barbara Cherry.
          p.   cm.
     ISBN 0-87605-984-1
     1. Poodles. I. Title.

SF429.P85C48 1994   93-23639
636.7'2–dc20   CIP

Macmillan books are available at special discounts for bulk purchases for sales promotions, premiums, fund-raising, or educational use. For details, contact:

Special Sales Director
Macmillan Publishing Company
866 Third Avenue
New York, NY 10022

10 9 8 7 6 5 4 3 2 1

Contents

The Poodle was originally used to retrieve game from water. However, the breed's intelligence and sense of fun make it ideal as a family pet.

*Barbara
Cherry
pictured with
Shanandi
Charley
Brown.*

About the author

Barbara Cherry has kept all three varieties of Poodles for twenty-five years, and has enjoyed considerable success in the show ring exhibiting her dogs under the Shanandi prefix. She is best-known for her Miniature Poodles, and honours include winning CC and Reserve CCs at Crufts, and Best Miniature Puppy at a Championship Show. She owns one of the top stud teams in Britain, and her puppies are in great demand both as foundation stock for show kennels and as companion dogs. Barbara is an International Championship Show judge, awarding Challenge Certificates in all three varieties of Poodle; she runs a large boarding kennel, and is a qualified dog groomer.

Acknowledgements

Thanks to the Guide Dogs for the Blind Association and to Roger Stone (Vanitonia) for the use of photographs.

Jacket photograph: Kelrama We've Done It Again Kertellas (pet name Tilly). Owned by Roger Bayliss.

Photography: Carol Ann Johnson

Chapter One

EARLY HISTORY

ORIGINS

There are a number of theories as to the Poodle's origin. It is certainly one of the oldest breeds recorded – there is a carving of a Poodle-type dog on a monument, dated approximately 30 AD, in the reign of Emperor Augustus. Greek and Roman coins have been found showing a dog resembling the Poodle, with a lion-like mane and hindquarters clipped short. Nearly all the early records show Poodles in traditional Lion trim, rarely in short trims.

THE POODLE IN FRANCE

The Poodle has had a colourful history in France, and there are claims that this is the breed's true country of origin because of its outstanding popularity in this country. French artists and engravers have depicted Poodles for many centuries, especially the small pet Poodles. Louis XIV had a small pet Poodle called Filou, who became a firm favourite, and this dog was featured in the work of several poets and novelists of this time. In fact, the French have played a major part in developing the pet Poodle as we know it today. Over a long period of time a small, slender type of Poodle, usually white, was seen in France. It was known as the *Petit Barbet*. The French like to claim that the Poodle is a direct descendant of the Barbet.

Other small Poodles have been depicted in France, including the *Caniche Nain*. This Poodle had soft hair, unlike the larger type Poodles. They were small in size, usually around twelve inches in height. Similar Poodles were also seen in Holland. A larger type of white Poodle, known as the *Mouton*, was seen in France, gracing the boulevards of Paris. There were also corded Poodles, where the coat fell in separate rope-like cords, intertwining top and undercoat, and these can still be seen in France today.

THE CIRCUS DOG

From the eighteenth century onward Poodles were used as entertainers. Some assisted clowns in their circus acts, others entertained in the streets in an early form of street theatre. In the early eighteenth century a large troupe of performing Poodles from France became the toast of England, performing highly unusual tricks such as tightrope walking, using their hindlegs, and racing with monkeys as jockeys. They performed all over England to enthusiastic audiences. In 1818 there is a record of a Poodle called Munito, who was supposedly able to do card tricks by counting! The French people recognized the Poodle's high intelligence and desire to please, and they began to train their dogs up to a high standard in Obedience.

THE WAR DOG

Moustache was the name of a Poodle who became famous for his bravery in war. He was born in Normandy in 1800, and he reputedly joined a regiment of the French Grenadiers and fought in the Battles of Marengo and Austerlitz. He gave the alarm as the Austrians approached, enabling his regiment to attack the enemy and emerge victorious. Moustache was rewarded with a decorated collar.

This was not the end of his exploits. A soldier carrying the Colours at Austerlitz was surrounded by the enemy, and Moustache ran to the rescue. The soldier continued carrying the regiment's Colours, but he was killed by an enemy bullet. Honour was at stake, and Moustache picked up the Colours and returned with speed to his regiment.

Unfortunately, he was killed in the Battle of Badajoz in Spain in 1811. He was buried on the battlefield with his collar and medal. His headstone had the inscription *"Ci git le brave Moustache"* – *"Here lies the brave Moustache"*. After the war the Spaniards smashed his headstone and burned the body of the dog. However, a wood-cutting survives, dated 1811, which shows Moustache in a continental trim, as we know it today.

THE TRUFFLE DOG

This was an inferior type of Poodle with an ability for scenting, and it was used to track down the gourmet's delicacy – truffles. The truffle is a small, round, leafless fungus found in beech woods from September to February. As early as Greek and Roman times, these delicacies were highly prized by gourmets, especially the French.

For centuries, pigs were used to scent out the truffles, but although they were skilled in finding them, they were also quick to root them up and devour them. The truffle-hunters would dash to the spot, shooing the pigs away, and trying to salvage the remaining delicacies. The Poodle would find the truffles, and would then stand over them, marking the spot, until the truffle-hunters came to dig them up.

THE POODLE IN GERMANY
THE WATER DOG

The French would love to think that they 'invented' the Poodle, but it is almost certain that the breed originated in Germany, where larger type Poodles were used as water dogs – 'Pudel' in German meaning to splash in water. These dogs appeared in sixteenth century engravings, showing two distinct styles – curly and corded. This Poodle-type water dog was probably of Spaniel origin, which was substantiated by descriptions of the water spaniel or 'water dogge' between 1400 and 1700.

This water dog would disturb the game, and then wait until his master arrived. In 1803 an engraving of a black and white mis-marked Poodle-like dog was found. The dog had a neglected Poodle-type coat and a shorter head than today's Poodle, but it had a marked resemblance to the Standard Poodle. In the late eighteenth century Poodles in France were depicted in paintings retrieving game from water.

THE BREED SPREADS

During the Revolutionary Wars the Poodle was carried by the troops into France, and during the later campaigns into Britain, Spain and Holland. Different types of

The Toy Poodle was evolved from the Miniature Poodle, and was recognised in Britain as a separate variety in the 1950s.

Poodles were seen in different regions, as the breed spread over northern Europe. Heavy, large Poodles were seen in Germany, and even larger Poodles, harnessed to carts, were seen in Belgium and Holland. In Russia a taller, more agile and elegant Poodle was seen, and this was usually black in colour.

Poodles were said to be used in Brussels for smuggling lace. To avoid heavy duties imposed on lace, Poodles were closely shaven and lace was wound round their bodies, before attaching a false skin, which was sewn into place. The dogs were thus able to evade Police and Customs officers.

Many other breeds have common ancestry with the Poodle; the Portuguese Water Dog and the Irish Water Spaniel both having distinctive Poodle-like coats. From *Canis familiaris aquatus*, the original water dog, the Poodle has progressed to become the elegant dog we know today, but it still retains the basic traits, such as its tremendous intelligence and sense of fun, which have made it so highly prized throughout its history.

THE POODLE IN BRITAIN

Although there are records of Poodles in Britain in the eighteenth century, it was not until the continental wars of the nineteenth century that the Poodle became established in Britain. The English Poodles were large crisp-coated water dogs, which were seen especially on the marshlands of north-east England. These large Poodles were used by professional poachers, and the dogs resembled the Poodles of today. The English Kennel Club had not been founded when Poodles came on to the scene. In 1876 the Poodle Club was founded by a group of ardent Poodle

Apricot Miniature Poodles: The Miniature was recognised as a separate variety in 1910.

enthusiasts. Formal recognition took place some years later in 1896. All Poodles at this time were said to be of unknown pedigrees. The Americans were becoming increasingly interested in the breed, and at the turn of the century the American and English Kennel Clubs started working together with the aim of breeding better Poodles. Many top-quality English Poodles were sent to breeders in America, and soon American-bred dogs were making the journey to Britain.

THE POODLE IN AMERICA

Most of the early Poodles around the late 1800s were large Poodles imported from England. They were found mainly on the east coast where several enthusiastic breeders lived. These Poodles were of a good type and were large. Miniature Poodles were also bred, but it took a long time for Poodles to become popular. The Poodle Breed Standard was drawn up in 1885 and the Poodle Club of America was founded in 1896 but dissolved in 1898. In 1931 it was re-formed. Interest in Poodles was much slower at this time in America than in England.

Some notable breeders at this time were Mr and Mrs Sherman Hoyt, Mr and Mrs Putman, Mrs Rogers and Mrs Marshall, to name just a few. Mr Price deserves a mention. He imported about six of the best Chieveley dogs following the death of Mary Moorhouse, the dedicated English breeder of black Miniatures.

Mr and Mrs Sherman Hoyt and Mrs Rodgers were responsible for importing many English dogs of note. One of the 'greats' imported by Mrs Hoyt was the outstanding white Standard dog, International Champion Nunsoe Duc De La Teracce. This dog was bred in Switzerland, exported to Miss Lane in the United Kingdom, where he was shown, winning everything in front of him. He sired many beautiful Standard Poodles in the United Kingdom before being sent to America, where he became a most influential sire. Mrs Hoyt and her fellow breeders continued to import many outstanding Poodles from England and other countries.

THE CORDED POODLE AND THE CURLY POODLE

At the beginning of the twentieth century, Corded Poodles were far more popular than the curly variety, especially for show dogs. The Corded Poodle's coat was never combed out, but strands were twisted with paraffin to form long cords. In approximately 1904 the corded and curly variety were divided by the Kennel Club into dogs over fifteen inches (Corded), and dogs under fifteen inches (Corded).

Many people believe that cords can be produced on any Poodle by not grooming the coats and growing the ungroomed hair to produce cords. There were arguments among breeders as to whether corded Poodles could be brushed out to become curly Poodles. Many breeders insisted Corded Poodles were not the same as Curlies. However, cords can be formed on today's Curly Poodles by growing and twisting strands of hair to produce cords. The Curly Poodle Club was founded around 1900. It stated that dogs shown as 'Corded Poodles' could never be exhibited as a 'Curly Poodle', and vice versa.

THE MINIATURE AND THE TOY POODLE

In 1910 Miniature Poodles were recognized as a separate variety. The stipulation was that they should not exceed fifteen inches at the shoulder. In 1926 Miniatures were reclassified and remained in the Toy Group for three years. They then became part of the Non-Sporting Group alongside Toys and Standards.

Lady Stanier was a pioneer in breeding small Poodles which were as good in all respects as the larger Standard type Poodle. She purchased a small white Miniature bitch and a Miniature white dog. She produced a litter containing a nine inch white bitch called Seahorses Snow Queen, who became the basis for a line of small, white Poodles which excelled in quality and intelligence. Lady Stanier line bred from Snow Queen (breeding from closely related offspring) to produce a recognizable type of Toy Poodle, possessing the small stature, yet retaining the quality of the large Poodle.

In 1957 the Kennel Club recognized the Toy Poodle in the United Kingdom. The American Kennel Club also gave the new variety formal recognition, but stated that the animal be no more than ten inches at the shoulder. The British Breed Standard for the Toy Poodle differed, stating that any Poodle under eleven inches at the shoulder could be registered as a Toy – even if it was the product of two Miniature parents.The British Toy Poodle Club was brought into existence by Lady Stanier who became the Chairman. Challenge Certificates were issued for the breed at Crufts in 1958 by the Kennel Club.

Two other leading Poodle enthusiasts at the turn of the century were Florence and Millie Brunker. They were originally interested in the larger-type Poodle, but then they became involved in breeding and improving the Miniature Poodle. Millie Brunker imported several excellent dogs from overseas, and with her expertise she used them to improve the Miniature Poodle.

Many famous blacks were bred under Millie's Whippendal prefix (kennel-name), and her clever breeding has influenced the development of the present-day Poodles of all three sizes. Her interest and her sister's extended to colours, especially apricots, silvers and blues. The true blue and silver dogs of today owe a lot to them both. Millie retained her interest in Poodles up to her death in 1943.

In 1912 Mary Moorhouse began breeding her famous line of black Miniatures under her Chieveley prefix. The famous Firebrave Poodles and many other famous black lines are descended from these dogs, and many of today's top Miniatures in the United Kingdom can be traced back to this line. Top-quality Chieveley dogs also went to America where they made a significant impact on the development of the breed.

Mary loved her little dogs, and she had decided views on breeding, line-breeding to produce a wonderful line of densely-coated, jet-black Miniatures. On her death in 1929 her entire kennel of Poodles passed on to her brother Sir Harry, who was unfortunately unable to cope with them. He selected a group of the best and sent them to Mr Price in America. The others were carefully rehoused, and those that were too old were put down.

Today all three varieties – Standard, Miniature and Toy – are highly-prized as show dogs and pets. The impressive-looking Standard finds particular favour in the show ring, but each variety has its band of enthusiasts. The Poodle really is a breed to suit people in all situations, and with its intelligence and lively sense of fun, it soon becomes a cherished member of its human family.

The Poodle is an athletic, soundly-built dog and can be trained to compete in agility competitions.

The 'Labradoodle': In the UK the Standard Poodle has been crossed with the Labrador Retriever to produce a highly trainable guide dog for the blind.

Chapter Two

CHOOSING A POODLE

The unique character of the Poodle is almost impossible to sum up. The breed is fun-loving, entertaining, faithful, friendly, intelligent, assertive and biddable.The Poodle is also the most versatile of pets, and his talents appear almost limitless. If you are about to embark on Poodle ownership, try to get acquainted with the breed by visiting a friend or a breeder with a Poodle or several Poodles. The true character of the Poodle can never be appreciated without being in close proximity with the breed. Once you have owned a Poodle, you will be happily hooked for life.

The Poodle thinks he is human! He adores his owner or family and loves to be included in all family activities. He will greet his owner after a short spell of absence with such enthusiasm, it is flattering. He can change allegiance from one person to another more easily than other breeds, and so if his owner is away he will attach himself to another member of the family.

Unfortunately, the Poodle has earned a reputation as a spoilt lap dog – bad-tempered and yappy – especially the two smaller varieties. This is not a true picture. A Poodle that is well-bred, well-disciplined and well-cared-for is a joy to look at and to own. He should never be aggressive, nervous or excessively yappy. These traits are alien to the Poodle.

Poodles are delightful pets, but think carefully before you decide which variety is best-suited to your lifestyle.

PHYSICAL CHARACTERISTICS

Physically, the Poodle is a good-looking, well-balanced dog. He also has a friendly out-going nature and a high degree of intelligence. Most Poodles are long-lived and have been known to live over sixteen years.

One of the major advantages of the breed is that they do not shed their coats, and as long as they are kept clipped, groomed and shampooed, they do not smell. They are one of the few breeds suitable for people suffering from asthma or hair allergies. Very occasionally an asthmatic may react to a Poodle, and if this happens it is doubtful whether such a person could ever own another dog. The Poodle coat can be a variety of colours, black, brown, white, cream, silver, blue, apricot and red.

Poodles are, generally, a healthy breed. They are very agile and have a lot of stamina – they are natural athletes and performers. Old people find smaller Poodles good pets as they are economical to feed and easy to lift and carry, making them ideal for those who live in apartments.

MENTAL CHARACTERISTICS

The Poodle is highly intelligent and quick and eager to learn. The breed can be trained to do a multitude of things. Poodles are capable of attaining high levels in Obedience training, although this is pursued more in America than in the UK, where handlers prefer the more conventional Obedience breeds such as the German Shepherd Dog. However, the Poodle has shown that it can excel in agility competitions, including mini-agility (for dogs under 15ins – 38cms), which have become very popular in the United Kingdom. Escava Black Extravaganza, a black Miniature bitch, owned by Jackie Carter, made breed history by winning top honours at Crufts mini-agility competition, and on the same day winning her second Challenge Certificate in her breed class. Poodles naturally balance on their back legs and are capable of pirouetting and jumping. They love the limelight and have performed for centuries as circus dogs.

In the UK Standard Poodles have been crossed with Labradors to produce a highly trainable guide dog for the blind. These dogs are known as 'Labradoodles'. This cross-breed combines the steady, gentle, willing nature of the Labrador with the extra height, high intelligence and eagerness to learn of the Standard Poodle. One of the main features of the Labradoodle is that it tends to shed very little, usually inheriting the Poodle-type coat. This makes the dogs suitable for asthmatics and for blind people with allergies to dust and hair.

Poodles are natural water dogs. They love swimming and retrieving. They are not often seen working as gundogs, but they would certainly be excellent in this field. The Poodle can be trained to scent. They are occasionally used in the United Kingdom to track down drugs for the Police.

A Poodle is too bright for his own good, and he can soon learn to manipulate his owner. It is therefore advisable to discipline your Poodle from an early age. He must fit into your life, rather than you fitting into his!

WHICH VARIETY?

Having decided a Poodle is the dog for you and your family, you must then consider which of the three sizes you would like to own, and, more to the point, which size you are able to accommodate and care for. The Standard Poodle is the largest of the Poodles. Standards must be over fifteen inches tall at the shoulder, and they usually range in height between twenty inches (51cms) and twenty-eight (71cms) approximately. In the UK a Standard under twenty inches in height will be too small to be shown successfully, and, ideally, it should not be bred from.

The Miniature Poodle is the middle-sized Poodle. The height at the shoulder is between eleven inches (28cms) and fifteen inches (38cms) in the UK; under fifteen inches and in excess of ten inches in the USA. The Toy Poodle is not more than eleven inches (28cms) at the wither (point of shoulder) in the UK, and up to ten inches (25cms) in the United States.

A Miniature-bred Poodle that grows to between fifteen and seventeen inches in height will not be classed as a Standard – merely an over-sized Miniature. A dog bred from Toy parents that reaches twelve to thirteen inches in height will be regarded not as a Miniature, but as an over-sized Toy. Toys were bred down from Miniatures, and the Toy Poodle was the last size to be recognised by the Kennel Club.

Occasionally a puppy will grow over the maximum height for its variety. This is perfectly acceptable for a pet, but not for a show specimen. If your puppy becomes grossly over-sized you can justifiably complain to the breeder.

THE STANDARD POODLE

This is a large, robust, active dog, bred originally as a water dog to pick up and retrieve game. He is not a suitable pet for the old or infirm, apartment dwellers or people in full-time work. The Standard will require one to two hours or more daily exercise, either walking on a lead or free exercise in a garden or park. A Standard puppy from eight weeks of age will need a certain amount of space to exercise his limbs and play freely. This is a necessary part of his development, mentally and physically.

A Standard puppy should not be left alone in a confined space for long periods. Boredom habits will develop, such as chewing and howling, and through no fault of his own, the puppy may become destructive. This does not mean he should not be confined for short periods with his own bed and belongings. This is part of his discipline and routine. If your space is restricted and you still want a Standard, you must ensure that you have plenty of time to dedicate to your dog, particularly during his youth.

The other option is to approach a breeder to see if any older animals are available. Occasionally, a breeder reduces stock and an older dog that cannot be shown or is unable to be bred from, or a bitch who has finished breeding, will become available. Most reputable breeders will let you have an older animal on a trial period to see whether you are both well suited. Make sure there is a trial before embarking on the older dog. Beware of the unsocialised kennel dog which has had only a little contact with the outside world and strangers, and possibly may not be house trained. If you have plenty of time, patience and stamina an older Poodle will soon get into your routine. The Poodle Rescue may be able to help you locate a suitable older dog, which needs rehousing either through a bereavement, marriage breakdown, or other circumstances.

A good Standard breeder will quiz you to find out whether you are a suitable owner for a puppy, making sure you understand exercise and feeding requirements. You should also take into account the costs involved in maintaining the coat. Anybody who sells you a Standard puppy without finding out whether you are

The Poodle adores his 'human' family and loves to be included in all activities.

Far from being a spoilt lap dog, the Poodle is self-confident, intelligent and interested in everything that is going on.

suitable is not a reputable breeder. The Standard Poodle is a large, active dog, and you should be aware of what you are taking on. Then, hopefully, your Standard will enrich your life and be part of your family for the next ten years or more.

THE MINIATURE POODLE

The Miniature is a suitable pet for most environments, and it will be less expensive to feed and clip. This variety does not require vast amounts of space or exercise, and a Miniature could live in an apartment, providing that he is given regular exercise. However, Miniatures can be lively, and they will certainly relish as much exercise as you are able to give. A Miniature puppy will need an area to play in while he is growing up.

THE TOY POODLE

Like the Miniature, the Toy is suited to most environments. He will live happily with old people, young people and children. However, if you have a family of boisterous youngsters a Toy could be at risk. He may be dropped or trodden on, and may be more likely to incur an injury. A Toy Poodle is more likely to break a limb than the larger Poodles, and that is why they should be supervised at all times when young children are about. The advantages of a Toy Poodle for the elderly are numerous. They are inexpensive to feed and less costly to clip. They can be easily picked up and carried and they do not need much exercise. They are also long-lived.

The final choice is yours. Think carefully and choose wisely. You cannot cast a puppy aside like an unwanted garment if it doesn't suit you!

WHERE TO BUY A PUPPY

Do not rush into buying a puppy from the man next door, just because it is a pedigree puppy. The best place to buy a puppy is from a reputable breeder. Contact your national Kennel Club, and you will be supplied with a list of breeders, or you will be put in touch with your local breed club. The breed club secretary will certainly be able to help you, and may even know which breeders have litters due. Alternatively, your vet may be able to help you find a puppy, as most practices deal with a number of different dog breeders.

In my opinion, the best way of buying the type of dog that particularly appeals to you is to attend a dog show, preferably a major show where many good Poodles are going to be on display. Look for a dog or dogs that you like, and then locate the owners or breeders of these animals by finding their numbers in the catalogue. Even if that breeder cannot supply you with a puppy, they will probably be able to recommend a suitable breeder that produces a similar type of Poodle.

CHOOSING A PUPPY

Do not go to a breeder expecting to have first pick of the litter. A number of the puppies may already be spoken for, and if you do not plan to show your Poodle, the breeder may be unwilling to sell you a puppy of outstanding show potential. However, whatever you plan to do with your puppy, you should expect to buy a nice, healthy typical-looking specimen of the breed.

For this reason, you should not rush into buying the first puppy you are offered. The puppy or puppies should be bright and alert, with clean healthy coats, bright eyes and clean ears. Ask to see the mother. She should be healthy, clean and friendly. If the mother is nervous or aggressive you should not entertain buying one of her pups. If puppies look thin, dirty, wormy or appear nervous, you would be advised to steer clear. A Poodle puppy should greet strangers enthusiastically, and should never cringe from you.

If you feel happy about the puppy that is offered to you – go ahead and buy it. You will receive a diet sheet, a pedigree and a registration certificate. Your puppy will have to be transferred to your ownership by signing this certificate and sending the applicable fee to the governing Kennel Club.

MALE OR FEMALE

As a long-standing breeder, I find it difficult to advise pet owners which sex to buy. I personally love my dogs (males), and I prefer to show dogs rather than bitches. Many people will advise you to have a bitch. It is often said that bitches are more faithful, but this is not necessarily true. I find Poodle dogs very loving and loyal. If you are looking for a companion, a dog is just as suitable as a bitch.

Dogs are usually less expensive to purchase, and they can be safely exercised all the year, unlike the bitch who has to be kept in during her seasons. I rarely find my Poodle males are over-sexed, although, unfortunately, Poodles have developed a reputation for this trait. If a male Poodle becomes a nuisance, clinging on to your leg or jumping on to other dogs, reprimand him firmly. If, over a period of time, this does not work the dog may need castrating. This will quieten him down, although it may also cause a weight gain. If a dog shows any aggression, castration may be the answer. Your vet will give you advice on this matter. A disadvantage of a male Poodle is the fact that he will show interest in bitches in season. If you happen to live next door to a bitch, you need to have a well-fenced garden, otherwise your dog will persistently stray.

Bitches are very loving towards their family and friends, but they can be withdrawn or over-excitable during seasons. A bitch comes into season at approximately six-monthly intervals. She will have a coloured discharge for approximately three weeks. Normally, she will keep herself clean by licking herself, but a little staining may occur on light carpets and furniture. She will have to be kept in your house and garden for the duration of her season. If she gets loose she may stray, as the urge to find a mate takes over at this point.

If you do not wish to breed from your bitch, and you do not want the nuisance of seasons, you can arrange to have her spayed. In most cases, your vet will advise you to wait until the second season. Spaying is costly, but is now a fairly straightforward operation. Once again, as with the castrated dog, a weight gain may result. However, a spayed bitch is less likely to suffer from uterine infections or tumours in later life.

A bitch may be given a contraceptive pill to suppress her season. This is not advisable over a long period of time as it can cause irregular seasons, weight gain, and tumours of the milk glands can occur. If you own another dog or you buy a pair of puppies, my advice is keep to the same sex. Poodles are delightful pets whether they are male or female – the decision as to which sex you wish to own is entirely personal.

The Miniature Poodle is a lively dog – but it does not need as much exercise as the Standard.

Poodle puppies should look bright and alert, like this litter of ten-week-old Miniatures.

The Standard Poodle is a large, active dog, and the new owner must understand the exercise and diet that an adult will require.

Chapter Three

PUPPY CARE

ARRIVING HOME

Try to arrange to bring your new puppy home during the morning, and this will give him time to adjust to his new surroundings before being left alone at night. Bedtime can be a traumatic experience when a pup has been used to sleeping with his littermates or his mother in his old home. The puppy will invariably become fractious – and very vocal – and will probably disturb the entire household.

If you can ignore these protests, do so. Most puppies will give in gracefully after an hour or so. If your puppy persists for a long spell, go to the door of the room he is in and scold him. Do not go into the room and pick him up – he will think he has won the battle. A ticking clock can be left close to a small puppy or a radio can be left on, and this may help to reassure the puppy at night.

HOUSING

Most Poodles are house pets, rather than kennel dogs. Your puppy needs to have his own corner, complete with bed, blanket and toys, which is free from household disturbance. The bed, plus bedding, must be placed somewhere that is free from draughts. It is inadvisable to leave a young puppy unsupervised, in a room with carpets and soft furnishings. Poodle puppies love getting into mischief – and the tassels on your best sofa are irresistible!

The kitchen or utility room is the ideal place to house your puppy, and it is a good idea to fence off an area of the room which can be used as your puppy's bedroom and exercise area. Low mesh panels are the most suitable for this job, but any other material can be used. Your puppy should be made to stay in this area for a few hours daily from an early age, so that he becomes accustomed to being left for short periods.

Indoor kennels are becoming increasingly popular in Britain – they have long been a standard item of pet equipment in the USA. They serve the same purpose, giving the puppy somewhere safe and secure to rest in. Make sure you provide your puppy with his favourite toys when you leave him, so he has something to distract him from chewing wallpaper, chair legs, or anything else that takes his fancy. Part of your puppy's 'exercise' area should be covered in newspapers, and most puppies soon get used to using this as a 'toilet' area.

Most small Poodles are total house pets and often sleep on their owner's bed, or in a basket in the bedroom. This is fine so long as everyone is happy with the arrangement, but remember that a Poodle will not take kindly to being shut in the kitchen if he has got used to sleeping in the bedroom.

BEDS AND BEDDING
I recommend buying one of the heavy-duty plastic beds, making sure it is big enough for the puppy to stretch out in, plus room to spare. These beds are not easy to chew and are hygienic and easy to scrub – they will be ideal for your Poodle. Wicker beds are attractive to the eye, but a large puppy may be unable to resist the temptation of chewing. The danger is that a pup may break off fragments of wicker which could choke him. Wicker also harbours dust and dirt. An older Poodle can be given a wicker bed, providing he is not destructive.

The ideal bedding for all puppies is the fleecy, washable material, which allows all moisture to soak through. It resembles sheepskin on a thick backing and it comes in several sizes. Buy a piece that is twice as big as your Poodle's bed, and cut it into two pieces – one to wash, one to use. If your puppy has an accident in the night the urine will pass through the fur fabric, and the pup will remain dry. This bedding also keeps the puppy warm. An old jumper or a garment, minus buttons etc. can be used for bedding, remembering that all bedding must be kept well laundered.

TOYS
These will be readily accepted by your Poodle. However, you must make sure you do not provide anything that is small enough to swallow, or where bits can be chewed off. Hard rubber dog toys, sterilised bones and chew sticks will keep your puppy out of mischief. An old knotted sock or thick knotted ropes are also much appreciated.

FEEDING BOWLS
Your puppy will need a good solid water bowl, preferably a non-spill type, available from most pet shops. I find stainless steel bowls are the most practical, as the plastic type chip and crack. They are also easily destroyed by a puppy's teeth. Your puppy's food can be served in a flat-bottomed bowl, again preferably metal. These bowls must be kept scrupulously clean.

COLLAR AND LEAD
There are plenty of puppy collars and leads on the market, and these are made of fabric, nylon or soft leather. These can be used on young puppies to train them to get used to wearing a collar. A leather, rounded collar is ideal for the adult Poodle, especially if it is in Lion trim. This type of collar will not rub the neck hair. Flat ornamental Poodle collars can be used as the puppy advances, once he is in a Lamb/Sporting trim, or any other pet trim.

GROOMING EQUIPMENT
You will need a firm brush such as a slicker brush (dense, short metal teeth on a flat base), which is available from most pet shops, or a bristle-type hairbrush. This will only be of use if your Poodle is groomed regularly, as it will not be effective on thick, tangled coats. A stainless steel comb will be needed to comb after brushing. (See Chapter 5: Coat Care.)

FEEDING
All breeders have their own ideas on feeding. Your puppy should be completely weaned and ready to leave the breeder at eight weeks – never before this age.

There is a wide range of collars and leads to choose from.

Indoor kennels are becoming increasingly popular with pet owners.

The flat, ornamental Poodle collar can be used as your puppy gets older.

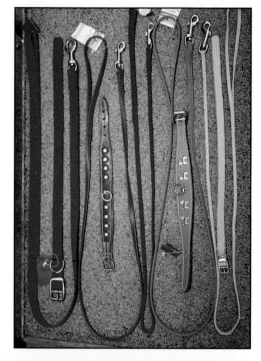

Stainless steel feeding bowls are recommended, as plastic or pottery bowls tend to chip and break.

Every breeder should provide the new puppy owner with a diet sheet, giving details of how to feed the growing puppy. At eight to ten weeks of age your Poodle will be on four to five meals daily. This diet should be adhered to for several weeks. New food must be introduced to the diet gradually. The general excitement of coming to a new home, meeting new people, and the change of water can upset a puppy's stomach, without the added stress of a changes in his food.

If your puppy does get an upset stomach, do not panic. The best policy is to reduce the puppy's meals for a day, and replace the meat with cooked chicken plus a little rice. Keep all food to a minimum for a few days and make the food bland. Hopefully, your puppy will make a swift recovery. It may be that your puppy refuses to eat for a day, or he may just pick at his meals due to lack of competition from his littermates. Again, do not worry unduly, your puppy will eat when he is hungry. Do not leave fresh food down for more than one hour. If your puppy refuses his dinner, remove it and feed him again in a few hours.

Most puppies will carry a roundworm burden. The breeder will have started off a worming programme, and you must ensure that you continue the treatment, otherwise your puppy will fail to benefit from the diet you are feeding. (See Chapter 9: Health Care.)

MEAT MEALS
By the time your puppy arrives home, he will be fully weaned, eating two meat meals and two cereal meals a day. I feed fresh food, top quality beef for dogs or minced cooked tripe, although a good quality brand of canned puppy meat is also suitable. I add fine wholemeal puppy biscuit, mixed in gravy or hot water, to the meat or tripe. Wholemeal bread can be toasted and crumbled into the meat for tiny Toy puppies.

ALL-IN-ONE PUPPY FOOD
There are numerous brands of 'complete' puppy diets available on the market. This type of food must be introduced gradually so as not to upset the digestion. The manufacturer's feeding guide must be strictly adhered to. These foods are completely balanced diets containing all the necessary nutrients to maintain your puppy's growth and all-round health. No additives or extras should be given to this diet as it could cause a dietary imbalance. Dried food is convenient for people working part-time, as food can be left down for the puppy to help himself when required, unlike fresh food which will become smelly and even fly-blown. Water must always be available when feeding dried foods. In my experience, large Poodles accept dried foods more easily than tiny Toy puppies.

DIET SHEET
(Suitable for Poodle puppies)
A guideline for puppy feeding is one ounce of meat per pound of body-weight, plus cereal.
BREAKFAST: Milk plus cereal or porridge. (I prefer to use goat's milk or evaproated milk as cow's milk can have a laxative effect on young puppies.)
MID-MORNING: Fresh meat, tripe, or canned puppy food or fish plus good-quality wholemeal puppy biscuit.
AFTERNOON: Repeat mid-morning meat meal.

EARLY EVENING: Scrambled eggs, egg custard or rice pudding.
SUPPER: Repeat breakfast.

If preferred, the afternoon and the early evening meal can be swapped, thus alternating the meat meals.

SUMMARY
The diet you feed your adult Poodle will be a matter of personal choice. Each dog is an individual as regards dietary requirements. If your Poodle puppy or adult is very active he may require larger amounts than average. If two puppies live together they may exercise more than a singleton. Their appetites will probably increase with exercise. Dogs that like a quiet life or placid puppies may not need the normal, recommended amounts of food.

Feeding is largely commonsense. Observe your dog's behaviour and condition and feed accordingly. Hyperactivity in puppies and adult Poodles can be caused by too high a percentage of protein in their diet. In this instance, review your Poodle's diet and make any necessary adjustments. Occasionally puppies reject certain foods. If this happens you will have to experiment, changing different parts of the diet. If your puppy has a permanently upset stomach, consult your vet.

HOUSE TRAINING
Poodles are not a difficult breed to house train. Even as young babies they will usually get off their bed and relieve themselves on newspaper, sawdust shaving or on concrete. Once your puppy has changed homes he will have to be taken at regular intervals to the designated toilet area. Every time your puppy wakes up he will automatically get up and sniff, circling to find a suitable spot to relieve himself. After feeding he will carry out the same ritual. At this point, pick your puppy up immediately or call him to come out into the garden, and wait until he has done his duty. Give lots of praise, and bring him back indoors.

If your puppy persists in running back indoors and soiling inside the house, reprimand him immediately and take him out to his patch. It may seem like an eternity waiting out in the cold for your pup to perform, but your patience will be rewarded eventually. If it is exceptionally cold or wet, and if you live in apartment, you may choose to let your youngster use newspaper, but this should only be done as a last resort.

If your Poodle wets on your carpet, blot up the worst of the puddle with paper towelling, and then spray the area with fizzy soda-water, or you can use a special preparation available from your local pet shop. This will remove the odour and staining.

INOCULATIONS
You will need to make an appointment with your local vet to have your puppy inoculated. Your vet will let you know at what age to start the inoculation programme, as this can vary from area to area. The puppy's mother should have been currently vaccinated for parvovirus, distemper and several other communicable diseases. The young puppies will receive the maternal antibodies via the bitch's milk, and they should be protected for approximately the first nine weeks.

Distemper has always been one of the worst canine diseases, but fortunately it is

All Poodles have a puppy trim until they become old enough to have a full trim. The coat will need to be groomed regularly.

If you are feeding dry food, as here, fresh drinking water must also be made available.

not as common in recent years as most people vaccinate against it. Parvovirus has been one of the biggest puppy killers, and it is only comparatively recently that an effective inoculation has been found. The virus can be transmitted on clothing, especially on shoes. It can be picked up from parks, dog shows and other places where dogs defecate. Your vet may blood test your puppy to see whether he has any protection in the form of antibodies to this disease. If there is no protection he will have to be vaccinated immediately. Vaccinating a young puppy that has protection will be useless as the antibodies in its system will inhibit the vaccine from taking effect.

Most dog vaccines are divided into two parts. The first inoculation is given at nine to ten weeks, the second is given about two weeks later. These give protection against distemper, infectious canine hepatitis, canine parvovirus, and leptospirosis. It may also cover parainfluenza, which is a highly contagious form of kennel cough, often transmitted from dogs kennelled together. An annual booster for these diseases will have to be given throughout a dog's life.

After vaccinations your puppy may have a rise in temperature and be off-colour for a day. If this persists, call your vet. Do not worm your puppy immediately after vaccinations, it is better to leave it for a week or so. In the United States your puppy should be vaccinated against rabies, with yearly or two-yearly boosters. If you observe your puppy appearing unwell and feverish, vomiting or passing blood, your vet should be notified.

SOCIALISATION

It is important to socialise your Poodle puppy as early as possible. This can start immediately after his vaccinations are completed. Your puppy should already be accustomed to normal household noises, such as doors banging and the sounds of household machines being operated. He should also be used to being picked up and handled by children (under supervision) and adults. Your puppy should also be used to his collar and lead. I find the best method is to leave a soft puppy collar on your Poodle for a day, and then attach a lead. Let your puppy walk round on his own to get him used to the feel of the lead, but watch him constantly in case he gets tangled in the furniture!

After a few lessons, gently pick up the lead and praise him. Follow the puppy wherever he wants to go. Finally, pull the lead gently and encourage your puppy to come to you, patting your leg and calling him. He may resist and fight against you like a bucking bronco. Wait for him to settle and try again. Once your puppy comes to you, give plenty of praise and reward with a tidbit, and gradually he will learn to follow you. If he resists again, squat down and encourage him, he will soon learn to accept the restriction of his lead.

Make these lead training lessons short. Start off by taking him on small walks to get him used to traffic, people, other animals, and the general hustle and bustle of life outside the home. The earlier your puppy is socialised, the more confident and well adjusted he will be as an adult. A puppy reared in a sheltered environment with only one or two people may become introverted if he is not taken out and about early enough in his life. Socialising your Poodle is largely a matter of commonsense on your behalf. If you introduce new experiences gradually, you will have a well-adjusted dog who will be a good ambassador for the breed, and a pleasant companion for you.

Chapter Four

THE ADULT POODLE

DIET

The three different varieties of Poodle mature at different ages. The Standard will not mature fully until approximately eighteen months, the Miniature between nine and twelve months, and the Toy earlier, at about seven months. Until this age, all three varieties will require more food than they will as adults, as they are still growing. There are numerous brands of canned, fresh and dried foods available for your pet, and you will need to find the diet that is best suited to your Poodle, and to your particular lifestyle.

ALL-IN-ONE FOODS: If you choose to feed an all-in-one diet, it is essential that you follow the manufacturer's feeding instructions. Some diets have to be soaked, others need to be fed dry. The golden rule when feeding this type of diet is to ensure that there is an adequate supply of fresh water available at all times. It is also important to remember that these are 'complete' diets, and no supplements should be added.

CANNED FOOD: A convenient method of feeding is to use canned food plus a quality biscuit meal. Once again, feeding quantities are explicit on the can. If your Poodle is not maintaining condition and body weight, increase his rations; if your dog is overweight decrease them. The quality of canned food does vary considerably, and you should make sure that you feed a good-quality brand.

FRESH MEAT AND CEREALS: The third way of feeding is fresh meat or tripe mixed with a good dog meal. I am a big advocate of this method. Biscuit meal is necessary with meat as it contains a lot of nutrients needed to maintain a healthy body. Meat or tripe can be fed raw or cooked. I like to cook a pan of meat and soak wholemeal puppy biscuits in the gravy, together with the meat. Even the smallest of Poodles will eat this with relish.

If your dog is hyperactive, he may be receiving too much red meat. In this case chicken or tripe plus biscuit will have to be substituted. Skin disorders are often caused by too much protein, red meat often being the culprit. There are no hard and fast rules to feeding. No two dogs have exactly the same metabolism. Lean, active dogs may require more food, fat lethargic animals need less. If your Poodle becomes obese, cut down on the cereal. Adult Poodles will be quite happy if they are fed once a day, although some people prefer to split the meal into two. Whether you feed once or twice a day, keep to a set time as your Poodle will welcome a settled routine.

EXERCISE

Puppies must not be over-exercised until they are fully developed physically, as damage can be caused by galloping excessively or by jumping on and off furniture. Exercise for the adult Poodle will vary according to the dog's size and temperament. Most Poodles will take as much exercise as they can get, especially when walked.

THE STANDARD POODLE: The Standard is a large, robust, active dog, originally bred to work to the gun. He will require at least one and a half hours exercise daily, walking or free running in a large garden or a park, especially while he is an adolescent. If your garden is small, you will have to walk your Standard daily. If you are lucky enough to own more than one dog they will receive enough exercise playing freely in the garden or in their run. However, a walk will still be relished.

THE MINIATURE POODLE: Again, this variety is robust and active, and Miniatures will take as much exercise as you are prepared to give, unless the dog is old or overweight. If you own a reasonable-sized garden, your Miniature will not need to be additionally road-walked, but any additional walks will be enjoyed.

THE TOY POODLE: This variety will not need hours of walking. A Toy Poodle can quite happily exercise himself in a small area, even by playing in the house. However, Toy Poodles will enjoy a walk. Never over-exercise a growing Toy Poodle or let him jump off great heights. They are more susceptible to limb disorders such as Legg Perthes disease (See Chapter 9: Health Care.)

TEETH

Your adult Poodle should have a full set of permanent teeth, numbering forty-two in total. They comprise of six incisors (small front teeth) on the bottom and top jaws, two canines (fangs) one each side of both top and bottom incisors. Behind each top canine are four premolars and two molars (total: twenty teeth). There are the same premolars on the bottom jaw, with an additional molar on each side (total: twenty-two teeth). The bite should be a scissor bite, with the top incisors lapping slightly over the bottom, and the fangs crossing tightly in the correct position.

Occasionally, milk teeth, especially fangs, will remain firmly implanted alongside permanent teeth. These should not be allowed to remain as they may cause the permanent teeth to come into the wrong position, which could affect the bite. If this happens, consult your vet, who will remove the milk teeth under a light anaesthetic. While your Poodle is teething, hard, large bones that will not splinter are helpful, as gnawing will help the milk teeth to fall out. Toy Poodles, in particular, sometimes retain a complete row of well-rooted milk teeth. If these remain for more than a few weeks after teething, consult your vet.

The Poodle's teeth, especially the Toy's, can cause problems. They need constant checking to make sure that tartar does not accumulate. Often Toy Poodles prefer sloppy food, and do not like chewing hard biscuits, chews or large bones. This causes the teeth to deteriorate. It is therefore a good idea to accustom your Poodle to having his teeth brushed from puppyhood. Specially manufactured dog toothpaste and toothbrushes can be purchased from a good pet shop. In fact, hydrogen peroxide will also serve to clean the teeth.

If tartar accumulates you can buy a tooth scaler. This has to be firmly inserted on

The Poodle should have a scissor bite, with the top incisors over-lapping the bottom incisors.

Tartar must not be allowed to accumulate on the teeth, and you may need to use a tooth-scaler to keep the teeth clean.

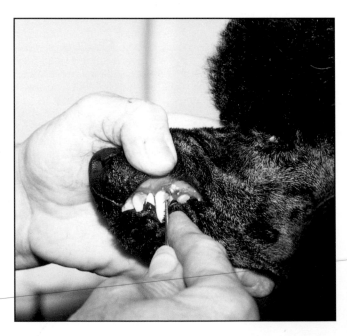

The Standard Poodle requires at least an hour and a half's exercise a day in order to maintain top-class condition.

top of the tartar next to the gum, and firm downward pressure must be applied. The hard scale will chip off. Gums must be regularly checked, and if they appear red and inflamed this could indicate an infection. If the teeth are clean, infection of gums is unlikely. Many pet Poodles object to their owners cleaning their teeth. This is less likely to be the case if your Poodle is used to the routine from puppyhood. If you encounter problems, be firm with your Poodle – if all fails, see your vet. He can give your dog a light anaesthetic, and then clean the teeth.

NAILS

A Poodle with correctly shaped feet – deep, tightly-knuckled and cat-like – should keep his own nails short if he is exercised wholly or partly on hard ground. Standards seem to possess better feet overall than the smaller varieties. However, pet owners often seem to allow nails to grow too long. I have seen talons projecting from the foot up to half an inch in length. This can be due to badly-shaped, flat feet with long toes that spread, and lack of exercise on hard ground.

Once nails have been neglected, it is not easy to cut them short again. There is a blood vessel running down the centre of the nail, and the nail must be cut back to the quick. If you cut the quick, the nail will bleed profusely. It is much easier to cut white nails as the quick is visible. It is therefore better to be cautious when trimming black nails. If you do cut the quick, apply pressure with your finger or a pad of lint or cotton-wool and apply potassium permanganate or a styptic pencil, and this will stop the bleeding. The aim is to get the quick to recede so that you can trim the nails short. After trimming, the regular use of a dog nail-file will help this process, coupled with road-walking exercise, which will wear down the nails. Your Poodle groomer will usually cut your dog's nails as part of the service. If you decide to cut them yourself you can buy a nail-clipper from a pet shop. I prefer the guillotine type, which slices quickly and efficiently.

PADS

Paws should be checked regularly for foreign objects lodged between the pads. Grass seed can become embedded between the toes, causing swellings. The seed may be plucked out with tweezers, and the sore area should be bathed in hot salt water. This problem can result in small cysts erupting between the toes. These are known as interdigital cysts, and they will require veterinary attention.

EARS

Poodles commonly suffer with ear problems, often referred to as canker. The hair that grows in a Poodle's ears should be plucked out every few weeks. You can do this by pinching the hair between finger and thumb and pulling. Ear powder can be applied to facilitate this, as the hair can be greasy. A healthy ear should be pink in colour, with no odour. If your Poodle scratches his ears, check them. Often there will be a distinct odour and a brownish deposit in the ear. This will probably be caused by ear mites, and you will need to obtain ear-drops from your vet. Ear mites are contagious from dog to dog, and they are often transmitted by cats, so you must ensure that all your pets are free from the problem.

It is a good idea to adopt a regular routine of cleaning out your Poodle's ears, using damp cotton-wool to remove any debris. I find that a little olive oil eases the cleaning process. Never probe into the ear with sharp or hard instruments. If the inner ear is inflamed it will be necessary to get veterinary advice. This could be caused by a deep-rooted infection needing antibiotic treatment, or it could be the result of a foreign object lodged in the ear, such as a grass seed.

EYES

Many Poodles, especially whites, suffer with runny eyes. This can be caused by blocked tear ducts, a foreign body or a draught. Constantly running eyes cause a brownish-pink discoloration. This can be unsightly. Eyes can be bathed in tepid water. Cold tea applied on cotton-wool is also supposed to be good for runny eyes, or you can buy a tear-stain remover from a pet shop. These remedies lessen the problem, but rarely provide a complete cure.

If you suspect there is foreign body in the eye and you cannot see it, consult your vet. Running eyes can also be caused by an ingrowing eyelash or eyelashes. This condition is known as entropion, and it may require corrective surgery. Any sign of pus or a greenish-yellow discharge from the eyes indicates an infection, possibly conjunctivitis. This will need to be treated by your vet.

ANAL GLANDS

Situated on either side of the anus are grape-like glands. These often fill up with an unpleasant, dark, foul-smelling fluid, which can be ejected when a dog is frightened. The smell is appalling! If your dog's glands appear puffy they will need emptying, and this can be done by you, your groomer or your vet. Often dogs that eat a lot of roughage empty their own glands when they pass a motion. If the gland is full and neglected, an anal abscess can erupt. This is painful for your dog.

Emptying the gland is achieved by covering the anus with a large pad of cotton wool. Squeeze with finger and thumb either side of the anal passage and apply pressure below the gland in an upward direction. The fluid will squirt out onto the pad. Be sure to empty the glands. The anus will need washing to remove odour. If your Poodle rubs his anus along the floor this could be because of an impacted anal gland or worm infestation. If in doubt, see your vet.

CARE OF THE VETERAN

As with old people, the old dog will need more cossetting than a younger edition. Generally, Poodles remain fit and active to a ripe old age. Even old dogs benefit from a small amount of regular exercise. The veteran may require two meals a day or several smaller meals to help digestion. Meat may have to be chopped more finely, and the biscuit meal should be more pulpy. The teeth will probably deteriorate rapidly. Your vet may have to remove some under light anaesthetic.

Make sure the elderly Poodle has a comfortable warm bed, well away from draughts. He will need letting out more often as his bladder may not be as strong as it was previously. His joints may become stiffer, and his eyesight will fail a little. This is to be expected. An aspirin per day will often help a dog whose joints are stiff.

Various problems may occur with the oldie, such as breathlessness often caused by heart trouble. Many oldies can go on for years on daily medication, even though they have heart trouble. You must be prepared to visit your vet more often with your old Poodle – he is worth it! If your veteran becomes really rickety and senile, make up your mind to put him to rest in a dignified manner. You owe this to him.

UK. Int. Swed. Nor. Ch. Racketeer Exquisit Sinner at Vanitonia shows off the Continental trim.

Chapter Five

COAT CARE

The Poodle possesses a unique coat, and is unlike most breeds that shed their coat twice annually. The coat of a Poodle will continue to grow unless it is regularly clipped and scissored to keep it tidy and in a good shape. If a Poodle's coat remains unattended it would continue to grow into ringlet-like cords. The majority of pet Poodles in the UK and the USA are clipped in the Lamb trim, also known in the USA as the Sporting trim, and occasionally the Dutch trim or Royal Dutch trim. These trims are the recognised pet trims, but modifications of these trims are often seen and are used for ease of maintenance. In the USA the Town and Country clip or a practical summer trim, known in England as the Clown Clip, are also used.

SHOW TRIMS IN THE UK
Adult Poodles in the UK can be shown in the traditional Lion trim (also known as the English Saddle trim), the Continental trim, and more recently the Scandinavian T-Trim. Some years ago the Lion trim was only seen on puppies, but now the fashion is to show Poodles of all ages in this trim. In special classes, such as Veteran, Brood Bitch, Stud Dog, Brace or Progeny, Poodles can be seen in Lamb trim. Puppies are normally exhibited in the Puppy Lion trim, but the T-Trim is now being used on some puppy exhibits.

SHOW TRIMS IN THE USA
An adult Poodle in the USA must be shown in the traditional Lion trim (or English Saddle trim) or the Continental trim, unless competing in Brood Bitch or Stud Dog classes, where they can be shown in a short Lamb trim known as the Sporting trim. Poodles over six months and under twelve months can be shown in the Puppy trim. Any other trim will be disqualified.

GETTING YOUR POODLE CLIPPED
Most pet owners with one or two Poodles favour having their pet trimmed at their local Poodle salon or grooming parlour, which will probably be advertised in the local paper or at the vet's surgery. Groomers can be located from local newspapers or specialised dog papers where they often advertise regularly. Failing this, ask another Poodle owner to recommend a good dog beautician who knows how to present a Poodle properly.

Your Poodle will need clipping at six to ten week intervals to keep him looking well. You may also bath and dry him between salon visits. You will need to give your groomer a few weeks notice before an appointment, or book your next appointment in advance. Good groomers are often fully booked and are in constant demand, especially in warm weather.

If you intend showing your puppy you will have to learn to prepare your dog yourself, otherwise it will be extremely costly and time consuming. Try to find someone who is experienced in the breed to either show you how to prepare your puppy for showing or who will do your initial shaping, giving you a pattern to follow.

If you own more than one pet Poodle you might find it too costly to have them trimmed professionally. My advice would be to take a few clipping lessons or attend a short course on clipping Poodles – these courses will be advertised in the dog papers. Some salons give lessons in clipping, and these may be costly as you are acquiring a skill enabling you to earn money clipping for other people.

GROOMING EQUIPMENT

The equipment you require is costly, and it is a false economy to buy cheap equipment. If you cannot afford such a large investment, try to pick up a good second-hand clipper, dryer and grooming table.

GROOMING TABLE: You will need a firm table with a non-slip surface for grooming and drying your Poodle. If your Poodle is a perpetual fidget you can purchase a stand to hook his lead on to, and thus prevent him from moving about.

CLIPPERS: These are an expensive item of grooming equipment, and there are a number of manufacturers who specialise in making them. Cheap clippers are a mistake, they are not usually designed for a heavy Poodle coat and will prove to be a waste of cash.

You will need at least two blades. The finer blade for face, feet and tail, and a coarser blade for the body. The finer blade often comes in different sizes, but you do not want anything too fine for a pet trim. If you trim too close to the skin your Poodle may develop a clipper rash. The body blades also come in different sizes depending on how long you want the hair.

NAIL CLIPPERS: There are several types on the market, the two most common being the guillotine and the pincer types. I favour the guillotine as it makes a clean quick cut, with no flaking.

DRYERS: The large power dryers are ideal for drying a Poodle quickly, but they are very costly to buy, and may be too expensive for one pet Poodle. You may start with a good quality hand dryer and a stand – this dryer will usually suffice for occasional use on a pet Lamb/Sporting trim.

COMBS: You will need a metal comb with fairly wide-spaced teeth, preferably with rounded teeth, not sharp spiky ones. Use your comb after brushing to remove any fine tags remaining. Never comb an unkempt coat – this will be painful for the dog.

SCISSORS: You will need a good quality pair of scissors designed for hairdressing. These can be purchased from firms advertising in the dog papers or from a hairdressing supplier. They come in a variety of shapes, weights and sizes, and vary considerably in quality. Ideally, a good-quality pair of stainless steel scissors about seven-and-a-half to eight inches should be purchased. Make sure you try out the scissors to see if they are comfortable to use, and they do not snag. Try not to drop your scissors as this will unbalance them, and have them sharpened regularly.

BRUSHES: A large pin brush or bristle brush, resembling a human hairbrush, should be used on the long hair, such as the mane of a Lion trim. You should brush from the roots to the tips, layering the coat. Use the brush firmly but gently so as not to damage the coat. A flat-backed brush with short metal pins, known as a slicker brush, should be used on short or matted hair. There are numerous brushes on the market, and the shopkeeper will advise you as to which is the most suitable.

POPULAR TRIMS FOR POODLES
PUPPY TRIM: Your young Poodle will arrive in a baby puppy trim. The face, feet and tail will be closely clipped and the other coat will be blow-dryed straight and shaped a little around the rear and the feet. Your puppy should be left in this trim for at least four and a half months, when he can be scissored into shape, or clipped into Lamb/Sporting trim. If you intend showing and you live in the UK, you will scissor your growing puppy into a puppy Lion trim until he is twelve months of age. American show puppies are shaped with scissors all over, but they are not put into 'pyjamas'.

CLIPPING FACE, FEET AND TAIL (ALL CLIPS)
THE FACE: The head must be firmly held with your hand over the skull, and ears held back to facilitate easy clipping of the head area. Keeping your clipper blade flat against the dog's skin, begin by clipping a straight line from the inner corner of the ear to the outer corner of the eye. For pet trimming do not use too fine a blade. If, after clipping, the skin turns pink or your dog scratches frantically you have clipped him too closely and caused clipper rash. Next time you clip him, clip with the direction of the hair on the cheeks and throat to leave the hair fractionally longer. Whites and light colours are more susceptible to clipper rash than black Poodles.

Lift the Poodle's chin up and begin clipping from just below the Adam's apple to the inner edge of the ear, making a triangular shape, being careful to keep the skin on the throat taut to prevent nipping of the skin. Hold the lips taut and clip along the sides of the muzzle and under the chin area, making sure the tufts of hair on the crevices of the lower lip are removed. Finally, clip from the stop (between the eyes) to the tip of the nose and clip against the hair in the crevices under the eyes to give a smooth finish.

THE FEET: Lift the foot and separate the toes by pressing your thumb on the top of the foot between the toes and your fingers underneath the toes. Using the corner of the blade flat to the skin, clip up one side of the toe and then up the other side, being careful not to nick the skin between each toe. If you feel unsure of yourself, clean out the hair on the base of the pads using your clipper, and then clip from the base of the foot at the rear of the foot for about half an inch above the ground.

THE TAIL: Clip about one-third of the tail towards the base, clipping towards the body, against the hair growth on the top, and with the hair growth around the anus

A chocolate Miniature Poodle in show Lion trim.

A chocolate Toy Poodle in Dutch trim – this is not seen very often as it is a difficult trim to keep in good order.

An apricot Miniature Poodle in second puppy trim.

This eleven year old Champion is kept in a 'puppy' trim with a short coat on the ears and tail for ease of management.

and underside of the tail, where the dog is particularly sensitive. The top two-thirds of the tail has longer hair which can be shaped with scissors into a round tail-pom.

LAMB/SPORTING TRIM

This is the most popular and practical clip for the pet Poodle or the breeding bitch, as it is neat and easy to keep clean and maintain. The face, feet and tail are clipped closely with a fine blade. The hair on the neck, back and ribcage is clipped with a coarser blade to leave a short curl, and the leg hair is blow-dryed and scissored into neat trousers. The face can be completely shaven or your Poodle can sport a moustache – there are three types to choose from. Firstly, the Donut Moustache, where the hair in the front of the muzzle is grown long from the centre of the nose with the hair combed downwards and with a long beard on the chin; secondly a short moustache comprising of scissored side whiskers but no beard; and finally a long moustache with whiskers and a beard but the top of the nose closely shaven. The choice is yours!

THE BODY: Clip behind the ears and the base of the topknot, down the neck to the wither, down the sides of the neck to the shoulder, and the front of the neck to below the Adam's apple. Clip the hair from the ribs and underside of the body using a blade designed for longer body hair and clip in the direction of the growth of hair. This is from head to tail. Begin clipping the side hair one inch from behind the point of the elbow. When clipping under the brisket pull the front leg forward to prevent the loose fold of skin being nipped. Lift the dog on to his hindlegs and clear the tummy area, using a finer blade. Do not go past the rear of the underside of the ribs.

THE LEGS AND TOPKNOT: Comb the hair out on the legs and shake each leg to let the hair fall naturally. Comb the hair downhill at the base of the foot and scissor a straight line above the knuckles of the feet. Shape the remaining hair with scissors, combing the hair outwards. The front legs should be fairly baggy and straight and the hair should be scissored to blend the longer leg hair into the shorter hair of the body. Follow the contour of the back legs, blending the hair of the legs on to the body hair. Comb the hair on the topknot outwards and scissor a line above the eyes, over the ears and at the back of the head, then shape the topknot with scissors to give an attractive ball shape. The ears are usually combed and the hair left long.

THE DUTCH TRIM

This is not an easy clip for a novice to carry out and it takes a lot of maintenance between trims. My advice to the pet owner is to keep your Poodle in Lamb/Sporting trim which is a short practical style, easy to shape and to follow. The Dutch clip is based on large fluffy legs with rounded shoulder pads and thigh pads on the rear legs. The hair is left long on the shoulder area tapering slightly on to the legs.

Begin making your pattern by scissoring or clipping a line from the base of the tail to the wither, the width of this line being approximately one inch. Clip this area with a blade designed for longer body hair; for a closer finish a finer blade can be used against the growth of the hair. Next, clip a band from the top of the back in the middle of the ribcage down the sides, about two-and-a-half inches in width in the case of a Miniature Poodle. These measurements are an approximation and can be increased or decreased according to the size of the dog, providing the proportions are kept balanced. Viewed from the top, the dog has a cross in the middle of his back. Put a loose collar on your Poodle's neck and let it fall into place naturally, and when you are sure of this position, clip or scissor the neck hair from the collar up the neck to the base of the topknot, working against the growth of the hair. The leg hair should be blow-dryed and completely free of knots, enabling you to begin scissoring the shape of the legs. The shoulder pads must be rounded off and tapered gradually to the legs. Viewed from the side, the shoulder area on a Miniature should be approximately six inches and the leg hair at the base about three inches in width. The hip pads are slightly smaller than the front ones and should be about five inches in width on a Miniature viewed from the side, and the leg hair down to three inches at the base. The topknot and tail-pom should be well-shaped, and the ears should be left long. The moustache is optional. The hair on the rear legs should follow the contour of the legs.

LION TRIM OR ENGLISH SADDLE TRIM

This is a must for all show Poodles and many pet owners like to see their dogs in this trim, but it requires a lot of maintenance. As with other clips, clip the face, feet and tail to give a smooth short finish. The rest of the long hair on the body and the legs should be blow-dryed straight. The coat needs to be at least three to four inches on the long areas, to be shaped into this trim.

Begin by parting the hair about two inches behind the last rib in the case of a Standard, less for a Miniature or Toy Poodle. Roughly cut the hair from the mane to the tail, and cut off some of the surplus hair from the legs. Stand your dog sideways and scissor the underside of the mane parallel to the ground, about one inch below the chest, being careful not to expose the elbows. Scissor a line horizontally about two inches from above the pastern, then comb the hair downwards and cut a horizontal line above the knuckles of the foot. Next, shave the area from just below the elbow to the scissored area above the pastern, this will leave an area of longer hair ready to shape into a front pom-pom.

You may now attempt the rear end. Start by standing your dog sideways with his back legs slightly back in an approximate show pose. Scissor a small thin band above the stifle joint and another about one inch above the hock, slanting the line downhill from the hock to the front of the leg. Turn your dog so that his rear is facing you and scissor the position of the lines for the poms so that both legs are even. Finally, shape the bottom and the middle poms and scissor the pack (that is the area from the back to the middle pom) into a rounded shape. To achieve a good shape you must watch other people trimming a Lion trim or demonstrating the scissoring techniques on your dog.

The mane must be combed outwards and left to drop naturally before you begin scissoring the final shape. From the back of the mane you will taper the mane towards the head and then round off the remainder of the hair to form a neat shape – this takes practice, so do not be too scissor-happy immediately. Finally, the hair on the chest must be cut shorter and blended into the mane. The top-knot must be put in with the use of rubber bands and backcombing techniques.

CONTINENTAL TRIM

This trim is very popular in America for all three sizes of Poodle, but in the UK it is usually only seen on Standards that are shown. The front legs are prepared in the

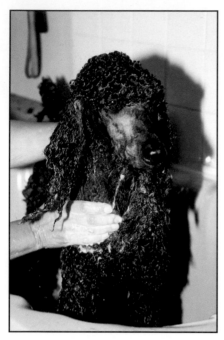

Before starting to trim, the Poodle is bathed.

A lead can be used around the body so that the Poodle stands steady on the grooming table.

The coat should not be clipped too closely for a pet trim.

The clipper is used between the toes. A finer blade is used for feet, face and tail, and a coarser blade for the body.

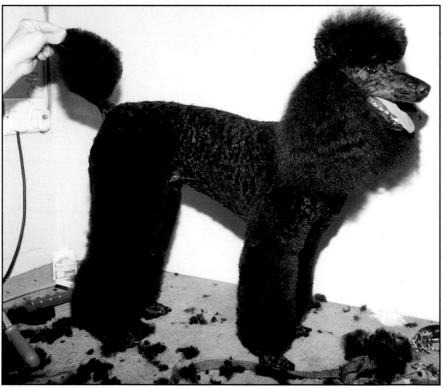

A Miniature Poodle in the Lamb or Sporting trim – the most practical trim for pet Poodles.

same manner as the Saddle trim. The hindquarters are shaved except for two rosettes one on each hip – although these are optional. Begin clipping a straight line on the back from the tail to the mane, this line being approximately one inch in width in the case of a Standard.

The rosettes should cover the hip bones and be rounded into shape using scissors. They should be positioned between the back of the mane and the point of the rump, making sure they are equal viewed from all angles. The remainder of the legs from the lower pom should be shaved cleanly. The mane need not be as large as that of a Lion trim, but it must be shaped in a similar manner. Once again this show trim needs a lot of practice to make perfect.

Chapter Six

TRAINING YOUR POODLE

Your Poodle will benefit from learning good manners and a little basic obedience, and he will soon become a pleasure to own. Teaching basic manners can begin from early puppyhood. A Poodle bitch will reprimand her puppies by growling if they step out of line. You must take over from her and keep your puppy in order. A Poodle learns quickly and has the ability to grasp several commands and retain them for the rest of his life. These early months are very formative ones when a puppy is developing physically and mentally. When training a puppy the tone of your voice is as important, if not more important, than the command. Each command should be administered in a different tone.

THE COMMAND "NO"
This is one of the most important commands for your Poodle to learn. From early puppyhood he can be firmly reprimanded with the command "No" when he is doing something untoward. If he persistently jumps up, chews furniture or barks, approach your puppy, push him down firmly or tap him on his rump, with the command "No". If he persists deal with him more firmly until he stops. If necessary, shake him by the scruff of his neck.

PRAISING YOUR PUPPY
When your Poodle obeys a command he must be praised, otherwise he will not distinguish between pleasing you and being disobedient. You cannot give a puppy too much praise when he has done the right thing; praise forms the basis of a happy working relationship.

THE RECALL
Your Poodle must learn from an early age to come to you when called. A dog that is totally disobedient is a nuisance to others and stands the chance of having an accident. A dog that is totally restricted and never allowed freedom will often run off or escape. A dog that is taught to come back to his call from an early age will trust his owner and not abuse his freedom. It is up to you to start his lessons as a baby, either in the garden or in the house.

Start off by calling your puppy's name together with the command "Come" i.e. "Pip, come". Keep your command light, never gruff or aggressive, or your puppy will think he is being scolded. When he comes to you, pat him and tell him what a good boy he is. Always praise him well, he will then want to please you more. If he fails to respond, make your command a little firmer. If he takes a few minutes or

Training sessions should be enjoyable for both dog and owner.

The correct way to put on a choke chain: the chain must run through the top of the ring so that it releases automatically.

Teach your dog to walk to heel on the left hand side.

The "Sit" is taught by giving the command and pressing the rump firmly with your left hand.

When you teach the "Down", apply pressure to the shoulders and, if necessary, give a sharp downward tug on the lead as you give the command "Down".

more to respond, do not be impatient with him – praise him when he comes to you.

THE "SIT"

This is another useful command to teach your Poodle. With your dog on your left hand side, raise his head with the lead using your right hand, and at the same time press his rump firmly with your left hand, giving the command "Sit". Make the command firmly and briskly. Your Poodle will quickly learn to respond to this command.

THE "STAY"

Put your Poodle on a lead and put him into the "Sit" position. Stand in front of him, raising your hand with your palm facing the dog and give the firm command "Stay", taking a few paces back from your dog. Do not speak or stare at him, unless he moves. You must then enforce the command by putting him back into the "Sit" position and giving the firm command "Stay" once again. Gradually, you can increase the distance, and increase the time until your Poodle can be left in one position for about five minutes. When he has completed his exercise, go back to him quietly and praise him.

LEAD TRAINING

If you have followed the advice given in Chapter 3 (Puppy Care), your puppy should now accept a lead and collar, and be walking reasonably at your side. You must now teach your Poodle to walk in an orderly manner. Many owners accept their pet hauling them along at the end of a lead, but this is no pleasure for the owner or for the dog. Your Poodle must be taught to walk without pulling.

If your Poodle continually pulls, give his lead a sharp jerk and give him the command "Heel". If after several attempts he does not respond, you will have to use a choke chain. The chain used should go round the neck with several inches spare to allow for movement.

With a Poodle in Lion trim, a chain may sever the neck hair, so it should only be used for short training sessions. The choke chain (or slip chain) must be put on correctly so that it releases immediately after jerking it. With your Poodle on your left side and a lead attached to the choke chain, walk forward and as soon as your Poodle pulls ahead, jerk the lead firmly to operate the choke chain. He should stop pulling, but if he lurches forward again, repeat the procedure. After several attempts he should stop pulling and walk quietly at heel.

SHOW TRAINING

If your Poodle is to be shown, you will have to attend show training classes. These classes will teach your dog to move at the correct speed, to do triangular and circular figures, to walk freely up and down and approach the judge in a confident manner. Your Poodle will learn to stand in a show position, showing off his virtues while the judge examines him. He will get used to having his teeth examined and his body handled.

OBEDIENCE TRAINING

Most owners are content to own a well-mannered Poodle that can be groomed and handled and respond to simple commands. If you wish to pursue obedience further, you will have to join a training club in your vicinity. These clubs are found in most towns and they advertise in local papers and veterinary surgeries, and will be known by local dog people. There may be a wait for classes as they are very popular.

It is advisable to take your puppy along before he is six months of age and watch the classes in progress. If you wish to join, enrol your puppy, he will not be allowed to officially train until he is six months of age. Some clubs now run special classes for puppies under six months of age, and your puppy can attend as soon as his inoculation programme is complete. These 'puppy parties' are valuable for socialising your Poodle.

When your puppy is six months old, you will probably be offered two types of training. Firstly, basic obedience to make your dog a good citizen, and secondly, more advanced obedience, suitable for competition work. How far you proceed is up to you and your dog, and your dog's ability. Basic obedience will include socialising your dog with others, learning the recall, walking to heel and learning to stay in the "Sit" and the "Down".

AGILITY AND MINI-AGILITY

These two types of obedience competitions are comparatively new. They require fit, fairly fast, alert dogs, together with a reasonably active and enthusiastic handler. Poodles love to perform tricks and love jumping, and so they are ideally suited to agility.

Provided your Poodle is reasonably fit and has a good outgoing temperament, he can be trained for Agility. Dogs are not allowed to compete in Agility until approximately twelve months of age, when they are physically and mentally mature. The dogs compete against a time clock, and they complete the circuit in a set time. If the dog takes too long, knocks down an obstacle, refuses an obstacle or takes a wrong turning, he will have penalty points added on to his time.

Equipment includes a steep frame with a plank going across to another steep frame. The dog has to scramble up the frame and balance along the plank, finally scrambling down the frame. Other equipment includes the tunnel, hurdles, the see-saw, the weaving poles and the suspended hoop (a tyre) and also a table for the dog to jump on and lie in a down position. Mini-agility is also becoming increasingly popular, with Miniature Poodles winning a good proportion of honours.

CURING BAD HABITS

FIGHTING

A group of male dogs will often have skirmishes to establish the pecking order or hierarchy. A pair of Poodles do not usually fight violently. They will often strut round each other and have a fight to establish who is top dog. The loser will usually slink away and avoid further confrontations with this particular dog. Two dogs can usually sort themselves out without interference from their owner.

If a nasty fight erupts, never put your hands around the neck or head to separate them, or you are in danger of being bitten. Get hold of the tail towards the base and pull the Poodle off his assailant. If possible, get someone to grip the second dog's tail to stop the fighting. A fight often begins with jealousy over a toy or the owner's affection. As a last resort a bucket of cold water thrown over the dogs should shock them into releasing each other.

A Standard Poodle masters the weaving poles, one of the standard exercises in agility competitions.

Your Poodle will enjoy the challenge of agility training.

It is essential for your Poodle to learn basic Obedience before advancing to competitive Obedience or agility.

CLIMBING ON TO FURNITURE

A dog, like a human being, will find the softest, most comfortable place to lie down, and that is often your bed or your best armchair. If you intend stopping this habit, start disciplining as early as possible. You must push your Poodle off the furniture and give a sharp command "Off" or "Get Off" or "No". Several reprimands should bring the necessary result.

BARKING

Persistent barking or yapping must be checked. Get out of sight when your Poodle starts barking, quickly enter the room and scold him giving the command "No". If he persists, repeat the exercise. Failing this, shake him by the scruff of his neck, again repeating "No". You must catch him in the act or he will not understand why he is being punished.

A dog usually has a meaningful bark if a stranger is around or somebody is at your door. Once the person is admitted, your Poodle must stop barking. If he persists, put him on a lead and quietly introduce him to the visitor – he will soon learn.

HANDLING

A puppy should be handled as early as possible, otherwise he may resent being held still and handled. If he is difficult, firmly hold him and reprimand him. He must accept having his teeth looked at, ears checked, nails trimmed, and any other sort of examination to enable him to be handled by a vet, or in an emergency. If an older dog becomes difficult he may require patient but firm handling to gain his confidence. If you cannot master your Poodle make sure he is muzzled before he sees a vet. This method is, however, a last resort.

TRAVELLING

Often young puppies salivate on their first journey. Ideally, a puppy should be taken on short journeys, preferably sitting on a lap, where he is less likely to be sick than if he is loose in the car. The sooner your Poodle gets used to travelling the better. Cover the car seat with an old towel and make sure the puppy is travelling on an empty stomach, and that he has been exercised to empty his bladder and bowels.

If your puppy remains unsettled, try small journeys to the park or somewhere that is pleasant for him. This sometimes works as the puppy associates travel with enjoyment. If he is still miserable and sick, you will have to use travel sickness aids. Never open the car windows wide in case he gets a chill or damages his eyes. An adult Standard Poodle needs a dog guard to prevent him lurching into the front in an emergency, or to prevent him jumping about and causing an accident. Dog harnesses similar to human safety belts are also available.

Chapter Seven

THE SHOW RING

Every recognised breed of dog has a Breed Standard compiled by the governing body, that is the Kennel Club in the UK and the American Kennel Club in the USA. The ideal dog is blueprinted in detail, point by point, and in the show ring the judges assess each dog against the Breed Standard. The Breed Standards used in the UK and in the USA are virtually identical, except for the sizes.

The UK states that Standard Poodles are over 15ins (38cms) at the shoulder, and Miniatures are under 15ins (38cms), but over 11ins (28cms) at the shoulder. The American Standard states that the Standard is over 15ins at the highest point of the shoulder, and any specimen below 15ins will be disqualified. The Miniature Poodle ranges between 15ins and 10ins at the shoulder (not 11ins as in the UK). Any Poodle which does not fit into this size range is disqualified. The Toy Poodle in America must be under 10ins at the shoulder, and any dog over this height will be disqualified.

Another difference between the two Standards is the description of the show trims. The British Standard states: "It is strongly recommended that the traditional Lion trim be adhered to." However, other trims are rarely penalised. The American Standard states: "Puppies under twelve months may be shown in the Puppy clip in all regular classes, Poodles over twelve months *must* be shown in the English Saddle or Continental Trim, except for Stud dog classes, Brood Bitch classes and Non-Competitive Parade of Champions, when Poodles can be shown in Sporting Clip. A Poodle in any other clip *shall* be disqualified.

THE SHOW POODLE

In my opinion, a good show Poodle must first and foremost possess an extrovert temperament. He must be well-balanced, carrying himself with dignity – he should never trundle along. His movement must be free and light, and he must cover plenty of ground. He must be of a good type, i.e. he must possess most of the good Poodle characteristics. Finally, he must be sound. This means that he must be constructed correctly, which will enable him to move correctly, viewed from any angle.

Whether a puppy or an adult Poodle, a good showman should immediately catch your eye with his carriage, his movement, his head and expression, and his profuse jacket. If you are offered a puppy possessing those attributes, give him further consideration! An experienced breeder can usually assess the potential of their own puppies, but may not be so accurate with puppies from different bloodlines. If you want a puppy for show, you will probably be offered a puppy of about eight to ten weeks with show potential. The pup has all the correct attributes to make a good

A dog must have the looks and the personality to be successful in the show ring.

A Poodle must be prepared for the show ring to show off his best points. This handsome white Standard is in traditional Lion trim (English saddle trim).

You must train your Poodle to stand squarely in front of the judge with head and tail held up. This Standard is being show in puppy Lion trim.

adult, and the necessary ancestry, but no one can ever guarantee that a puppy will become a top show winner. Occasionally, a promising puppy may grow too tall or remain too small or develop some ugly fault, which will preclude him from the show ring. You may purchase a well-bred specimen, who is good enough to compete and win at minor shows, but not quite up to Championship competition. This dog can be used as your training ground for showing. You can learn to prepare and show your Poodle making the best of his good points. Show him at small shows to gain experience, then you can decide whether to try and breed your own show puppy or, alternatively, buy a better specimen. This first Poodle will have taught you a lot.

THE BREED STANDARD
Both the United States and the United Kingdom Breed Standards require the following points:

CHARACTERISTICS: An elegant, active and highly intelligent dog with a square build, well proportioned, carrying himself proudly and able to move soundly.

HEAD: Long and fine with flat backskull (that is with flat cheekbones and flat muscles to the side of the skull). The stop (the indenture between skull and foreface) should be moderate and the distance from the occiput (dome on the top of head) to the stop should equal the distance from stop to nose. The muzzle should be fine, long, fairly strong and chiselled (it should have shaping under the eyes). The lips should be tight, never loose, and the chin should be well-defined. There should be forty-two teeth, white and strong, and the bite should be a 'scissor bite'. The head should be in proportion to the rest of the body.

EYES: Dark and oval in shape, set moderately well apart with an intelligent, fiery expression.

EARS: Long, wide, set low, hanging close to the head with thick long fringes (featherings on ears).

NECK AND SHOULDERS: Neck of a good length and well proportioned, strong enough to carry the head high, with no loose skin at the throat. The shoulders should be well laid back and be strong and muscular. The legs should be set straight from shoulders and be well muscled.

BODY: The length from breastbone to the point of rump should be equal to the distance from the highest point of shoulder to the ground. The chest should be deep and quite wide (not narrow between front legs), the ribs should be well sprung and rounded. The back should be level except for a slight hollow behind the shoulder. The loin should be short, muscular and broad.

TAIL: Set on quite high, thick at root, docked at a correct length to give a balanced appearance.

HINDQUARTERS: Well-muscled thighs, stifles (knees) well bent. Hocks well let down. Hind legs straight and parallel viewed from the rear.

FEET: Fairly small, tight and oval in shape, toes arched, thick hard pads with plenty of cushioning. Short nails.

FRONT LEGS: Straight, parallel when viewed from front. Elbow to be directly below point of shoulder. Strong pasterns, bone and muscle in proportion to dog, never spindly or weak.

COAT: Dense and harsh in texture, thick and curly. In the United States Corded Poodles are described as having tight, even cords of varying length, longer on mane or body than elsewhere.

COLOUR: Any solid colour. Blacks, whites, creams, silvers and blues, should have black points, that is, black lips, eye-rims, and nose, and black or self-coloured toenails and very dark eyes. Apricots should have dark eyes and preferably black points, but the liver coloured nose and eye-rims are permitted. Browns (chocolate) and Cafe-au-lait (light-browns) have liver points and dark eyes (never yellow or staring). Particolours (patches of colour) are not permitted.

GAIT: Free light springy action with plenty of drive from hindquarters, the movement to be sound and effortless. Head and tail carried high.

SHOW TRAINING

Puppies should attend show ring training classes and learn to stand quietly to enable the judge to examine their teeth, body and coat. Miniatures and Toys must learn to stand on a table; Standards are assessed on the floor. A puppy must learn to move freely on the handler's left hand side, moving fluidly and turning correctly.

The Poodle should learn to stand squarely in front of the judge, with his head and tail up. The dog must also learn to be stacked, i.e. presented by the handler holding the dog's head in the correct position, placing the legs correctly and holding the tail in the right position, to enhance the shape of the dog. The two smaller varieties must learn to stand still whilst the judge carefully lowers a measure over the top of the shoulder, if indicated.

It is lovely to see a Poodle moving on a loose lead, although initially this is difficult to achieve with an exuberant puppy. At no point should the handler stand between his dog and the judge. The judge will want a clear view of your dog at all times.

TRIANGLES AND MOVEMENT

You are often asked to do a 'triangle'. This entails you moving your dog on your left hand side in a triangular shape, with the apex being at the judge's end. This figure enables the judge to see the side view, the rear view and front view of your dog while moving.

You will also be asked to move your dog up and down, keeping your dog on the left hand side and at an even pace. This should be a smart walk for small Poodles and a faster pace for the larger exhibits. At the end of the mat you must turn round and walk in a straight line towards the judge. Do not drag your dog round at the end, causing him to be off balance and break his rhythm. If you are handling a Standard, turn him on your inside in a small U-shape. In the case of a Miniature or Toy, you can turn at the top and change hands, i.e. take your dog up on your left

Your Poodle must look immaculate for the show ring. Some exhibitors protect the featherings until the dog is ready to enter the ring.

The Toy Poodle is examined on the table, and is measured to ensure it does not exceed the correct height. This Poodle is being shown in puppy Lion trim, acceptable for all ages in Britain.

The show dog must get used to being examined by the judge. This Toy is in traditional Lion trim.

and bring him down on your right. Your Poodle must approach the judge and stand alertly and squarely in front of him. If he drops his tail at this point you will have to set him up (stack him) for the judge to look at.

SHOW EQUIPMENT
If you decide to show your Poodle on a regular basis you will need some basic items of equipment. This includes a secure travelling crate big enough for your Poodle to stand or turn in. A table with wheels which folds down to accommodate your crates and dogs is essential. The top of the table needs a non-slip rubber mat on it. You will need a grooming bag with all the grooming gear, hair-sprays and bands, plus a lead and collar and a water container. The advice of an experienced exhibitor regarding equipment or 'tack' will be of tremendous value to you.

THE DAY OF THE SHOW
There are different categories of shows, and it is advisable to start off in the smaller shows and work up to competing in the big Championship shows. Details of shows, and classes can be obtained from your Kennel Club.

On the day of the show make sure to arrive early enough to settle you and your dog down. Your Poodle will need a walk after his journey and possibly a drink of water. You need to get to the designated grooming area, erect your table and groom and scissor your dog and prepare his top-knot for exhibition. Go to your allocated ring in plenty of time, keep cool, calm and collected. The ring steward will give you your number and tell you where to stand.

Concentrate on your dog at all times, never let him sniff other dogs and be a nuisance. Keep him alert in case the judge is watching. Listen carefully to the judge's instructions and keep calm, then hopefully you may receive your first prize!

Chapter Eight

BREEDING POODLES

It is a fallacy to listen to those who say "it will do your bitch good to have a litter". If she was purchased as a companion, why have a litter? To breed unnecessarily or to mate your Poodle bitch to the Poodle next door is foolhardy. Dog breeding should be undertaken by knowledgeable breeders who have studied pedigrees and who know the faults and virtues of two animals, and not by a complete novice.

RESPONSIBILITY AND EXPENSE
It is a big responsibility to breed, rear and find suitable homes for a litter of Standard Poodles or a large litter of Miniatures. Standard litters often exceed ten puppies; Miniatures often have over five puppies. To rear a large brood will involve considerable expense, and a lot of time.

The bitch needs to be given good-quality meat, cereal and milk food from the midpoint of pregnancy and for the first three or four weeks after the birth to enable her to lactate well and nourish her growing puppies, and her rations will be considerably increased. Large litters (over eight puppies) may have to be supplemented, which will entail regular bottle-feeding, day and night. Between three-and-a-half to four-and-a-half weeks the puppies will begin to take solids, and only the best-quality lean meat, chicken or fish should be given. By eight weeks of age a Standard litter of ten puppies will be eating you out of house and home, and cleaning up after such a litter is very time consuming.

WHELPING COMPLICATIONS
If your Poodle is unable to deliver a puppy normally, she may need a Caesarian section, which is costly and occasionally risky. Poodles can sometimes react badly to anaesthetic. Your orphan puppies will have to be hand-reared if a foster mother cannot be found. This entails feeding every puppy at two-hourly intervals, both day and night, using a special bottle. Believe me, you will need stamina for this! You will also need to take over the mother's role, stimulating the puppies to pass urine and a motion after feeding (with the aid of cotton-wool soaked in warm water), and you will have to keep the puppies clean.

SELLING THE PUPPIES
At six to eight weeks of age, you will need to start looking for homes for the puppies. This may entail advertising, and this can be costly, particularly if you have to run several adverts. Each prospective purchaser must then be strictly vetted to make sure the home is suitable, especially in the case of a Standard. Make sure the

When a bitch is due to be mated, she should be in a pet trim that will be easy to cope with when she is whelping her litter and feeding her puppies.

If you are a novice breeder do not dabble in mixing colours. A white-bred dog should only be mated to a white or cream bitch.

Good temperament and sound construction are vital if you are planning to breed from your Poodle. This dog is a natural extrovert with a delightful disposition.

prospective owner has enough room, and is prepared to give sufficient exercise, otherwise you will end up rehousing an unmanageable puppy. If you are breeding for commercial gain – forget it. If you breed and rear correctly, you will probably just about break even.

YOUR FIRST LITTER

I may seem to be totally against a novice breeding a litter – this is not so. If your bitch is well-bred, a reasonable specimen of her breed with a good temperament, no known hereditary defects, and you feel capable of breeding, go ahead. Never breed from a nervous or aggressive bitch. These traits are alien to the Poodle and are likely to be inherited by some of her pups. If she has an hereditary problem such as hip dysplasia or slipping patellas, she should not be used for breeding. Never hesitate to seek advice from a more experienced person. Breeding good dogs is a skill, not a matter of luck, and a knowledge of pedigrees and genetics is needed, plus a great deal of common sense. There are three methods of breeding: In-breeding, out-crossing and line-breeding.

IN-BREEDING: There are various degrees of in-breeding. For example, father to daughter, mother to son, and the closest of all, brother to sister. This close breeding leads to a uniformity of type, as little new genetic material is introduced. Providing both animals are good specimens their dominant characteristics should pass on to their offspring. However, in-breeding doubles up on unfavourable traits as well as favourable traits, and these faults will pass on to future generations. A half-brother to half-sister breeding, which is not so close, may be less risky.

OUT-CROSSING: This involves the mating of two animals that are not closely related, where there is no common ancestor within at least three generations on both pedigrees. The offspring will probably be a mixed litter of different shapes and sizes. These animals are unlikely to produce offspring that resemble themselves when mated.

LINE-BREEDING: This is based on breeding when there are one or more common ancestors quite close in the two pedigrees. These ancestors pass on their good points to the majority of offspring. This method is good for perpetuating a favourable characteristic – a type of animal recognised by certain good points. Most breeders advocate a certain degree of line-breeding with an occasional out-cross to bring in new genetic material. Line-breeding should never be undertaken by a novice.

FINDING A SUITABLE STUD DOG

When you decide you want to mate your Poodle, the first step is to contact the breeder of your bitch. Do not wait until the bitch is fully in season as it might be too late to use the dog of your choice. A good stud dog is often booked for several weeks in advance.

In my opinion, a Poodle bitch, especially a Standard, should be at least eighteen months old (and in her second season) before producing a litter – preferably older. Under this age, the bitch is usually mentally and physically immature. Your breeder will help you select a dog suitable for your bitch, weighing up the faults and virtues of both animals. Good temperament and sound construction must be paramount in choosing a stud dog, however glamorous he may appear to be.

If your bitch's breeder is unable to help you locate a suitable stud dog, you can contact your Kennel Club for a list of breeders in your area, or you can look at the stud advertisements in the dog papers. Secondly, if your breeder is unobtainable you can phone the Kennel Club who will be able to give you the name of another breeder in your area.

The owner of the stud dog chosen will advise you to test for any hereditary abnormalities that are present in your breed. In the case of Miniatures and Toys, you may have to produce a clear eye certificate from a qualified ophthalmic vet. In the case of Standards, you may be asked to produce hip X-rays of your bitch, as hip dysplasia is an hereditary condition. The stud dog should also be tested for hereditary defects.

THE CHOICE OF COLOUR IN POODLES

It is inadvisable for a novice breeder to dabble in mixing colours. Blacks should be mated to blacks to produce blacks, and occasionally browns if both parents carry a recessive gene for the colour brown. A brown and a black can be safely mated together. You may get an all-black, an all-brown litter, or a litter containing both colours, dependant on the genes involved.

To be sure of producing an all-brown litter, brown must be mated to brown. No other colours should be produced from parents possessing only black and brown ancestors. Likewise, a white-bred white should be mated to a white or a cream, with no coloured ancestors close in the pedigree. Apricots and silvers should be mated to dogs of the same colour, providing other colours have not been used in the pedigrees. If both of the pedigrees contain mixed colours you may get a litter containing puppies of several colours and sometimes a mis-marked puppy with white patches on the chest, head or paws. These mis-marks must not be registered or bred from – they are pets only!

WHEN TO MATE YOUR BITCH

Your bitch's season (oestrous) lasts for approximately three weeks. The first signs of a season will be your bitch becoming excitable and flirtatious with other animals. Her vulva will start to swell and become obvious when viewed from the rear. She will start losing a pinkish discharge. At this point, contact the stud dog owner to arrange the approximate day of mating.

Watch your bitch daily; she will lose a red-coloured discharge after a few days, and I begin counting from the first day she loses colour. It helps if you bed your bitch on a white sheet, and then you will not miss the first day of losing colour. On approximately the tenth or eleventh day of season, the colour of the discharge will subside to a pinkish-brown. The vulva will be soft and very enlarged. This is the time for mating. The exact day will vary from bitch to bitch. If you feel unsure of her readiness, tickle your bitch around her tail, she should turn her tail sideways and lift her vulva in readiness for mating. She should go to the stud in ample time.

THE MATING

A pet bitch may resent advances from a strange dog, and she may need to be muzzled and firmly held so as not to hurt the dog. The dog will mount the bitch and

A Miniature Poodle pictured at ten days old.

Poodles make good mothers, and for the first couple of weeks, the bitch will feed and clean up after her puppies.

When you are rearing a litter you must use top quality food.

A nice, evenly-matched litter of apricot Miniature Poodles at ten weeks.

Good rearing is the key to producing a healthy, well constructed puppy. This pup has just had his first trim, ready to go to his new home.

after penetrating the bitch with his penis, the two animals will tie. At this point his penis will swell within the bitch's vulva and her muscles will tighten. They are then tied and will remain so for up to forty minutes or more until the bitch's muscles relax, releasing the dog. A few minutes after the tie the dog will turn and stand back to back with your bitch. After mating, the dog may be sponged down and your bitch sat on a clean towel. If the tie is satisfactory one mating will probably be sufficient. The stud owner may suggest a second mating forty-eight hours later – if his dog is available. Remember your bitch can still be mated for another week or more, so keep her in to make sure she is not mated by another dog. Otherwise she could produce a mixed litter from both sires. If your bitch is mismated, consult your vet.

PREGNANCY

This lasts for approximately sixty-three days. Your bitch will need worming during the first few weeks if she has not been treated before her mating. She should not receive extra food or cossetting for the first four or five weeks. At five weeks, food rations can be increased. Early signs of pregnancy at approximately this time will be the enlargement of the teats which may become pink, especially with the maiden bitch. Older bitches may not exhibit this sign until six weeks.

At five weeks the bitch's rations should be increased by about one-third, divided into two meals. By eight weeks increase food by one-half, divided into several small meals. Bitches carrying a large litter may require more food – but not fattening foods. Additives are not needed, in my opinion, providing the existing diet is well balanced with a good-quality meat plus cereal. Milky food can be included, but generally it is better to increase the meat (protein) rations rather than the cereal (carbohydrates). Exercise should be light, with no galloping after six weeks, and preferably no bumpy car rides during the last week.

THE WHELPING BOX

A special whelping box should be available for your bitch to whelp and rear her puppies in. If you do not want to purchase one, you can construct a wooden box with three high sides, and a lower side to enable the bitch to jump in and out. It is a good idea to put a sliding hatch or panel in the gap when the puppies are growing, and beginning to clamber.

In the case of larger Poodles, the three high sides should have guard rails. Guard rails are pieces of wood (broom sticks are ideal) fixed about four inches from the ground, and about four inches in from the three sides of the box. This ensures that if a bitch lies on a puppy it will not be crushed between her back and the wall.

Puppies cannot retain their body heat and so they must be kept warm, at a constant heat for the first few weeks of their lives. The room temperature needs to be 80 degrees Fahrenheit overall (27 degrees Centigrade) or an infra-red lamp can be suspended over the pups to keep them warm – be careful not to have the lamp too low or they will burn. It is advisable to prepare for the whelping by collecting plenty of clean newspaper, and assembling clean towels, sterilized scissors and cotton wool.

Your Poodle should be introduced to her box well before the whelping date, otherwise she may decide to have her pups in your bed, the garden or somewhere else undesirable. Just prior to whelping, remove the hair from the underside of your Poodle and make sure her rear end is clean and free from excess hair.

PROBLEMS DURING PREGNANCY

Any sign of discharge during pregnancy, other than a little clear liquid, should be an alarm sign. Discharge that is brown, green or red spells trouble and you should consult your vet immediately. It may only be a slight infection which can be cleared by using antibiotics, or it may mean that the bitch is losing her puppies. Abortion usually takes place in later pregnancy, usually around seven weeks. Partly-formed puppies can be aborted, or can be passed as a discharge from the vulva.

Occasionally a bitch will appear to be pregnant outwardly. However, as a result of stress her body will re-absorb the puppies. There may be no outward sign, although often the remains pass in the urine. This can occur at any time during the pregnancy.

WHELPING

Most bitches will whelp on time or up to a week early. If your bitch goes over forty-eight hours from her expected date, consult your vet, this could be the start of trouble. The first sign that whelping is imminent is when the bitch starts scratching up the paper in the whelping box, and she may refuse food a day or more before the birth. Just prior to whelping her stomach will drop as the puppies move into position ready for birth, and her temperature will drop to below 99 degrees Fahrenheit (37 degrees Centigrade). Her vulva will enlarge considerably and will become sticky.

Your bitch may lose water from her vulva if the water sac bursts prior to the birth of the first puppy. She will pant frantically and begin contracting. During contractions, your bitch will strain and her back will be seen to ripple. Her efforts will become stronger at each contraction, and these will be repeated at short intervals until the puppy is expelled. Often a brownish bubble will appear from the vulva, a further contraction will usually cause the puppy's head and shoulders to appear, finally the whole puppy will emerge, plus greenish-brown fluid. If the water bag bursts prior to the birth of the pup, the pup will be born without a sac.

Most pups come covered in a tough membrane, which you must break if the mother does not. Do this immediately. The bitch may lick the pup vigorously, clearing its nose and head area. If not, you must clear its airways, using your little finger, and rub and shake the pup to remove any fluid in the nose and mouth and airways. The bitch will normally chew the umbilical cord close to the puppy's navel. If she does not do this you will have to break the cord. This can be done by compressing the cord about one inch from the puppy, using clean fingernails, which will cause it to break. Alternatively, you can tie a piece of cotton in the same position, and then cut the cord with sterilized scissors near to the cotton, always cutting above the cotton, furthest away from the puppy.

Usually the afterbirth appears with a short contraction, attached to each puppy by the cord. If the afterbirth does not arrive after the cord is severed, it will probably appear at the birth of puppy number two. If the afterbirth is not passed and the puppy is still attached, do not pull it unless the bitch contracts. The bitch can be allowed to consume several afterbirths if she wishes. They contain many valuable nutrients. In the case of a large litter, try to remove a few if she lets you. Afterbirths should be counted. If any are retained the vet will give the bitch an injection. If this is not done she will run a temperature and become listless and ill.

If your bitch strains for more than one hour, or if contractions stop, call your vet immediately. If a puppy becomes jammed, carefully grip the pup and gently rotate it while the bitch contracts. Never pull if she is not contracting. If a puppy becomes totally jammed, you must seek veterinary help without delay. If this is your first litter, it is advisable to have your bitch and puppies checked by your vet. He may choose to give your bitch a calcium injection. He will check each whelp for any abnormalities, such as a cleft palate. If there are abnormalities these pups must be disposed of.

CARING FOR THE NURSING BITCH AND PUPPIES

Your bitch must be given plenty of fluid to bring her milk in. For the first forty-eight hours keep her on a light diet of milky foods, fish or chicken, never red meat – this contains too much protein. The milk should come down within twenty-four hours of the birth. If the puppies are fractious and the milk is not flowing freely, you will have to dropper-feed each puppy with special fortified milk, using an eye-dropper or a puppy feeder. The milk and feeder can be supplied by your vet. However, in most cases, the bitch will have plenty of milk for at least three to four weeks of the puppies' lives. Large litters may need additional supplementation to help your bitch.

Make sure your puppies and the mother are warm and dry. Puppies should suckle as soon as they are born and the litter should be quiet and contented. A puppy will double its birth weight at just over one week. If some puppies are not thriving, you will have to supplement them. The puppies will need docking at three to four days, and this should be carried out by your vet. Dewclaws should be removed at the same time. At approximately ten to fourteen days the puppies will open their eyes, and at about fourteen days their ears will open. You will need to maintain an overall temperature of 80 degrees Fahrenheit (27 degrees Centigrade) for the first three weeks.

The puppies will walk unsteadily at about three weeks of age, and by five weeks they will be completely mobile. Their milk teeth will appear in the gums towards the fourth week. By three to four weeks, solids can be introduced to the pups in the form of fine raw meat. Small amounts initially, and after a few days two meals can be introduced. Different foods must be introduced gradually, such as fortified milk, cereals and other meat or tripe. By six weeks of age the puppies should be almost independent of their mother, and they should have had their first worming treatment. By eight weeks they should have their second worming and be totally weaned, receiving five meals per day. Your bitch's milk should now dry up quite quickly.

Chapter Nine

HEALTH CARE

A healthy dog is a happy dog, and it is up to you as a responsible owner to keep your Poodle in tip-top condition by regularly checking him to be sure everything is in good order. A lot of health problems can be avoided by early diagnosis, prevention being better than cure. Your Poodle must be fed a good-quality, well-balanced diet. Many Poodles suffer from obesity due to overfeeding – often too many tidbits between meals. Obesity triggers off a multitude of disorders such as heart trouble, breathing problems, limb problems, diabetes, and occasionally skin trouble. If your Poodle is underweight, with projecting ribs and a staring coat, he may need worming, a better diet or more food, or it may be something more serious. Lean dogs are normally fit and healthy and usually outlive the obese specimens. Food should be given at a regular time, and should never be followed by violent exercise.

Hygiene is essential when caring for animals, and your Poodle should be regularly groomed and bathed when necessary to keep his coat and skin in good condition. Eyes, ears, and nails should be checked regularly. Your Poodle needs a warm, dry sleeping area free from draughts, and bedding should be regularly laundered. All water and feeding utensils should be kept scrupulously clean.

EXTERNAL PARASITES

FLEAS
These are the most common parasite to be found on your pet. The odd flea can be picked up from almost anywhere, however clean you keep your dog and your home. Fleas are at their most active in summer and autumn. The flea is the intermediate host of the tapeworm, which makes it imperative to keep the flea under control.

If your Poodle has fleas he will start to scratch. On closer examination, you will see black gritty particles on the skin. It is not always easy to see the fleas as they move quickly and jump. The flea is small, shiny and a reddish-brown in colour, and usually congregates on the head, the stomach and the base of the tail.
TREATMENT: If possible, wash your Poodle in a good insecticidal shampoo, and repeat the bathing as necessary, according to the instructions. Flea powder or a spray can be used, again following the manufacturers' instructions and repeated as necessary. All bedding should be disposed of, if possible, otherwise it should be well laundered and sprayed, and baskets should be thoroughly disinfected and sprayed with flea spray. A flea collar can be put on your Poodle. The collar is impregnated with insecticide and remains effective for several months. If a flea collar causes any skin irritation, remove it immediately.

LICE

Lice are pinkish-grey in colour, small and spherical and they are commonly found on the hair inside the ear-flap, especially on long-eared breeds such as Spaniels and Poodles. They can be found on all parts of the body attached to the hair, where they lay eggs (nits). The eggs stick to the hair and resemble particles of scurf, often going undetected. On close examination, the eggs are seen to be shiny and hard. They hatch out and small lice go to the skin where they suck and bite. Unlike fleas, lice move slowly.

If your Poodle persistently scratches his head and ears, examine him thoroughly, especially around the ear edges. Lice, like the flea, can be the intermediate host of the tapeworm. In the case of young puppies, lice can be dangerous if unattended, causing anaemia, or even death.

TREATMENT: Louse shampoo, obtained from your vet or pet shop, is needed to wash your Poodle, following the manufacturers' instructions. If possible, shave the hair from the affected area (especially inside ears) to remove the nits and facilitate easy treatment. Any dogs in close contact with your pet should also be treated.

TICKS

Ticks are usually picked up in country districts, especially on sheep pasture. Often they can go unnoticed until a small sore erupts. On close examination you may see a greyish sac attached to your dog's skin by a headpiece with suckers. After feeding, the body sac fills up with blood and becomes pink, large and engorged, often up to quarter of an inch in diameter.

TREATMENT: Apply cotton wool, soaked in surgical spirit, and then remove the tick with tweezers, making sure that the head is removed. If not, an infection will set in, often resulting in an abscess.

RABBIT FUR MITES

Excessive scratching, with no visible signs of anything on the skin other than a little dandruff, may indicate the presence of mites. They cannot be observed with the naked eye. Your vet will examine the skin through a microscope and if mites are present he will prescribe a special shampoo. Ordinary insecticidals may be ineffective with fur mites.

HARVEST MITES

As the name indicates, these mites are present at harvest time. They are only just visible to the naked eye and are reddish in colour. They burrow into the dog's skin, especially between the toes. Special veterinary shampoo must be used.

INTERNAL PARASITES

ROUNDWORM

Most puppies suffer in their early days from roundworm, even if wormed regularly. Healthy puppies can vomit or pass worms. They are pinkish in colour and resemble small earthworms, sometimes up to six inches long.

SYMPTOMS AND TREATMENT: Listlessness, dull coat, runny eyes, distended stomach, coughing or vomiting or loss of weight. All or several of these symptoms may indicate the presence of worms. There are many effective wormers available, both safe and easy to administer.

TAPEWORM

Tapeworm mainly affects the adult dog, and it is often transmitted by an intermediate such as the flea or louse, also rabbits and birds. A dog may pick up and eat a flea or may eat part of a dead rabbit or a carcass containing tapeworm larvae. SYMPTOMS AND TREATMENT: Loss of or increased appetite can be the first signs of tapeworm. The dog may rub its anus along the floor if it is wormy. Occasionally, white mobile particles can be seen in the faeces and dried white particles seen around the anus.There are special preparations in liquid and tablet form available from your vet or pet store. It is necessary to see that the head comes away with the rest of the worm to rid your pet of the tapeworm.

HOOKWORM

Hookworms are not common in the UK. They are blood-sucking worms, causing a drop in your dog's body weight. A vet will have to diagnose and treat these parasites.

HEARTWORM

These are worms affecting the heart tissue of dogs. Heartworm rarely is seen in the UK. It mainly occurs in hot climates and is common in the United States. The heartworm is transmitted by the mosquito. It can be serious if not treated early. Veterinary advice needs to be sought. Blood testing can be done annually to be sure of your dog being clear of heartworms.

INOCULATIONS

Your puppy should be vaccinated for the major diseases: distemper, leptospirosis, canine parvovirus, and infectious hepatitis. Your vet may also give an inoculation for kennel cough. In the UK, dogs do not need an inoculation for rabies, but this is required in the USA and many parts of Europe. Your vet will advise you as to the exact time to vaccinate. Annual booster vaccines must be continued throughout your dog's life.

COMMON AILMENTS

ABSCESSES: Your Poodle will feel off-colour and lethargic due to a painful swelling containing pus. While the abscess is developing he will feel very low and will probably run a temperature. The abscess will fill up with pus until it is hard – it will then erupt, discharging pus and a little blood. Abscesses are usually caused by bites, grass seeds or some foreign body embedded in the skin. A skin abscess will need to be bathed in hot water and salt or an antiseptic to help draw it so it will eventually burst. Keep bathing it with warm water several times daily to help the pus to clear.

BREAKS: If you suspect your Poodle has broken a limb, try to immobilize him and keep him warm. Gently feel down the limb. If your Poodle screams when you are feeling the limb, or if there is any heat or swelling present, this could indicate a break or sprain. If you have to carry your dog, make sure you support the affected limb, and get him to your vet as soon as possible.

BURNS: Soak the affected area in cold water. If possible, trim away any hair

A healthy dog is a happy dog, and with good care, regular exercise and a well-balanced diet your Poodle should enjoy a long life.

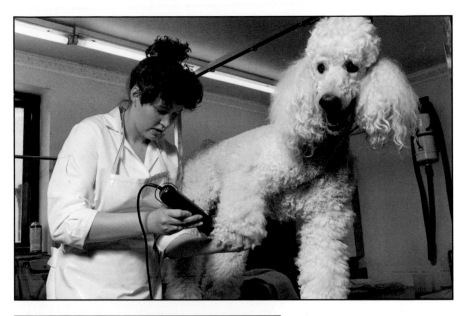

ABOVE: Your Poodle must be kept groomed and trimmed, and this will help to avoid parasites and skin problems.

LEFT: Obesity can lead to many health problems, so keep your Poodle well exercised and do not fed him too many tidbits.

around the burn. Your dog will probably be in shock – keep him warm and call a vet.

CONSTIPATION: This is often caused by bones, resulting in the faeces becoming hard, but it may be through an incorrect dietary balance. If your dog strains for a while and eventually passes a motion, check his next bowel movement. If he continues to be constipated give a mild laxative available from your vet or pet shop. Your vet may suggest a change of diet.

COUGHING: A slight cough or gulping may be the onset of Tonsillitis. Open your dog's mouth and if either side of the throat appears to be red, or phlegm is present, this could be the start of Tonsillitis or Kennel Cough. See your vet who will prescribe antibiotics, if necessary. Children's cough medicine, such as glycerine, honey and lemon can be given to your dog. Older dogs may cough after exercise through a defective heart. Puppies or older dogs may cough, indicating the possible presence of worms.

CYSTS: A cyst is similar to an abscess, and it may cause little or no trouble. These are known as Sebaceous Cysts. They occur on the skin and, providing they cause no trouble, they may be left. If they are excessively large or they burst, see a vet.
Cysts are common between the toes (interdigital cysts), and are often caused by a foreign body, such as a grass seed, embedding itself into the skin. Bathing in warm salt water or antiseptic will usually cause the cyst to burst, releasing the foreign body and accompanying fluid. If the cyst becomes infected, see a vet for antibiotic treatment.

DIARRHOEA: This is caused by some toxic matter in the system. Diarrhoea can be caused by parasites (worms), foreign bodies, change of diet, stress, over-eating, or something more serious. Starve your dog for twenty-four hours except for boiled water and a little glucose. After a day, introduce a light diet such as a little chicken, rice or fish. If the dog remains loose after forty-eight hours of this treatment, see your vet who will investigate further.

FITS: Occasionally, an apparently healthy puppy will have a slight convulsion, often frothing at the mouth and wetting itself. Stay with the pup and keep him quiet and warm. Be careful not to get bitten. Puppy fits can be caused be over-heating, over-excitement and teething. Often this puppy fit will be an isolated episode, and will never recur.

EPILEPTIC FITS: Epilepsy affects mature animals and is hereditary. It will vary in the degree of severity and regularity, but will be almost sure to continue for the rest of the dog's life.

HAEMORRHAGE: This is usually a heavy blood loss from a vein that is damaged, where blood is seen to be dark red in colour. This type is easier to stop than arterial bleeding, when bright red blood spurts from the wound.
Do not bathe the wound. Apply a pressure bandage over the wound, tie it firmly and leave in place until a vet is contacted. With bad arterial bleeding from a limb, a

tourniquet (such as a clean cloth or handkerchief) should be applied above the bleeding point (head-side). Do not leave a tourniquet on for longer than ten minutes – this is an emergency and a vet must be located.

LAMENESS: This can be due to a variety of reasons. Examine the pads for cracks, cuts, or foreign bodies.

Remove any foreign body, if possible, and disinfect. If the pad is cut, bathe in warm water and a mild antiseptic. If the cut is deep, bathe it and put a gauze pad over the foot, then bandage halfway up the leg to secure the pad. If possible, the whole foot should be enclosed by a bandage (not too tight).

If the pad appears sound, run your hand down the affected limb from the shoulder to the ground. If there is any heat or swelling, or the dog cries or winces, it could be a strain, sprain or break. Your vet will have to be consulted.

Lameness may also be due to rheumatics, a hip problem, Legg Perthes Disease, Patella Luxation or ligament or tendon trouble, to name just a few. Your vet will be able to accurately diagnose the problem.

PHANTOM PREGNANCY: Some bitches have a phantom pregnancy, and this happens after a season. This can be stressful for the bitch, particularly if it becomes a common occurrence.

The bitch will usually become restless and sometimes irritable, often scratching up bedding, carrying toys around and acting out of character. This condition involves enlarging of the breasts and secretion of milk, and it can last for up to a few weeks. Try to distract your bitch by removing her toys and taking her out and about. Usually the bitch will return to normal within a few days. If the condition persists you will have to seek veterinary advice.

RASHES: Small or large red pimples usually on the stomach area. A rash is often caused by an allergy to food, disinfectant or another substance. Your vet will try to find out the cause which will often need antibiotic treatment.

STINGS: A sting in the mouth will cause swelling and will require veterinary examination, as antihistamine will be needed. If a bee has stung and the sting is visible, remove it with tweezers and apply cotton wool on a clean pad. Occasionally dogs develop allergic reactions to stings and will develop blotches or will swell up excessively in the region of the sting. If this happens, seek veterinary help.

VOMITING: This usually occurs if a dog has eaten something that has upset his stomach. If a dog vomits once or twice, rest his stomach for at least half a day. Feed only a light diet, plus water. If vomiting is persistent, it may be the result of worms, poison, or the beginning of a more serious complaint. Seek veterinary advice.

WOUNDS: Small cuts and abrasions can be bathed in antiseptic. Your Poodle will probably then lick the wound. If the wound is in thick hair, clean round the wound carefully with warm water and cut off any matted hair. If the cut is deep, cover with a pad and secure the pad; the cut may need stitches. Puncture wounds such as from a nail or bite are painful. They will require bathing in antiseptic, and a visit to your vet, who will probably prescribe antibiotics to fight infection.

HEREDITARY DEFECTS IN POODLES

PATELLA LUXATION (SLIPPING STIFLES)

This is only found in Toys and Miniatures. It involves a severe weakness in the knee joint where the knee slips out of joint. Occasionally the dog will limp and after a few minutes the joint will right itself. In bad cases the condition will have to be operated on. It is inadvisable to breed from dogs with slipping Patellas, as it runs in families.

LEGG PERTHES DISEASE

Again, this is found in small Poodles, invariably started by the puppy jarring or knocking itself whilst growing. Certain lines have a predisposition to this injury, but many vets have difficulty in finding out accurately how it is passed on. The top of the femur is damaged, causing a lack of blood supply to the joint. The bone then degenerates and this causes acute pain and lameness. If the puppy is rested, almost immobilised, the joint will improve, but more often surgery is necessary. Legg Perthes Disease usually appears between five and twelve months of age. An affected dog should not be bred from.

PROGRESSIVE RETINAL ATROPHY (PRA)

This is a problem in Miniature and Toy Poodles, where the retina degenerates, sometimes slowly, sometimes quickly, causing eventual blindness, which is inoperable. All breeding dogs and bitches should be tested annually from twelve months of age, to determine whether the dog has the start of this disease.

ENTROPION

This is a condition where the eyelid turns inward causing the eyelashes to damage the eye. If this is not corrected by surgery, permanent damage can be done to the dog's sight. Dogs with severe Entropion should not be bred from.

JUVENILE CATARACT

This used to be common in Standard Poodles, but it seems to be less prevalent today.

HIP DYSPLASIA

This is more common in large breeds, including Standard Poodles, but is now becoming more prevalent in Miniatures. It has a complicated mode of inheritance due to a series of genes, and is influenced by the way the Poodle is fed and reared. It often results from problems in youth when the bones are growing rapidly, and over-feeding, over-supplementing and over-exercise are factors in the development of the condition. A dog with this complaint is usually very lame and has difficulty in getting up and trotting around for any length of time. Sometimes a growing puppy will appear lame but the condition seems to right itself and the animal becomes sound. These individuals will usually develop arthritis in later life.

Severe dysplasia will require surgery, and this is costly. It is advisable to have your Standard Poodle X-rayed and scored before breeding, and if the results are poor, the animal should not be used for breeding.

Dear Parents:

Congratulations! Your child is taking the first steps on an exciting journey. The destination? Independent reading!

STEP INTO READING® will help your child get there. The program offers five steps to reading success. Each step includes fun stories and colorful art or photographs. In addition to original fiction and books with favorite characters, there are Step into Reading Non-Fiction Readers, Phonics Readers and Boxed Sets, Sticker Readers, and Comic Readers—a complete literacy program with something to interest every child.

Learning to Read, Step by Step!

Ready to Read   Preschool–Kindergarten
• big type and easy words • rhyme and rhythm • picture clues
For children who know the alphabet and are eager to begin reading.

Reading with Help   Preschool–Grade 1
• basic vocabulary • short sentences • simple stories
For children who recognize familiar words and sound out new words with help.

Reading on Your Own   Grades 1–3
• engaging characters • easy-to-follow plots • popular topics
For children who are ready to read on their own.

Reading Paragraphs   Grades 2–3
• challenging vocabulary • short paragraphs • exciting stories
For newly independent readers who read simple sentences with confidence.

Ready for Chapters   Grades 2–4
• chapters • longer paragraphs • full-color art
For children who want to take the plunge into chapter books but still like colorful pictures.

STEP INTO READING® is designed to give every child a successful reading experience. The grade levels are only guides; children will progress through the steps at their own speed, developing confidence in their reading. The F&P Text Level on the back cover serves as another tool to help you choose the right book for your child.

Remember, a lifetime love of reading starts with a single step!

Copyright © 2021 by Tad Hills
Text by Elle Stephens
Art by Grace Mills

All rights reserved. Published in the United States by Random House Children's Books, a division of Penguin Random House LLC, New York.

Step into Reading, Random House, and the Random House colophon are registered trademarks of Penguin Random House LLC.

Visit us on the Web!
StepIntoReading.com
rhcbooks.com

Educators and librarians, for a variety of teaching tools, visit us at RHTeachersLibrarians.com

Library of Congress Cataloging-in-Publication Data is available upon request.
ISBN 978-0-593-18122-5 (trade pbk.) — ISBN 978-0-593-18123-2 (lib. bdg.) —
ISBN 978-0-593-18125-6 (hardcover) — ISBN 978-0-593-18124-9 (ebook)

Printed in the United States of America
10 9 8 7 6 5 4 3 2 1

This book has been officially leveled by using the F&P Text Level Gradient™ Leveling System.

Rocket
Has a Sleepover

Pictures based on the art by Tad Hills

Random House 🏠 New York

Rocket is happy!

He is having a sleepover
with his friends.

The friends play
hide-and-seek.

They eat snacks.

Later,
they say
good night.

But Rocket
is not tired.
He can not sleep.

"I will tell you a story," says Fred.

"There once was a puppy
who loved to swim."

"One day,

he met a frog."

"Then what?"
asks Rocket.

Fred falls asleep!

Rocket is not tired.
"I will finish the story,"
says Owl.

"The puppy and the frog
had a race."

"Who won?" asks Rocket.

Zzzzz . . .

Now Owl is
asleep!

Rocket is not tired.

"I will finish
the story,"
says Bella.

"The frog got tired
and needed to rest!"
says Bella.

"The frog called for help."

"The puppy was
about to win
the race."

"Then what?"
asks Rocket.

Now Bella

is asleep!

"Oh no," says Rocket.
All his friends
are asleep.

"I will finish
the story,"
he says.

"The puppy
went back."

"He helped the frog."

"They finished
the race together,"
says Rocket.

"The frog and the puppy
were tired."
Rocket yawns.

"They found a blanket
and fell fast asleep.
The end."

Rocket is tired.

He falls fast asleep.

The end.